38

JACQUES-ALAIN MILLER is head of l'École de la Cause. A fine writer and mentor, he is the sole editor of Jacques Lacan's works. He teaches at Paris VIII—and dictates a yearly Seminar *Orientation lacanienne*, at the Théâtre Dejazet, Paris.

ALAIN BADIOU teaches at Paris VIII and is Conference Director at the Collège International de Philosophie. An English version of his *Second Manifesto for Philosophy* was just published (Polity).

ÉRIC LAURENT is a French psychoanalyst. Member of the ECF, he has a Parisian private practice. A headmaster of the Freudian Field, he is a celebrated lecturer and writer. He teaches at Paris VIII.

MARIE HÉLÈNE BROUSSE is a practicing analyst, member of the WAP and of l'École de la Cause freudienne. She is the Editor at *Cultural/ Clinical Lacan*, and her writings are published in the ECF journal.

PIERRE-GILLES GUÉGUEN, is a French psychoanalyst. A member of l'École de la Cause freudienne and of the World Association of Psychoanalysis, he teaches at the Sorbonne in Paris.

LILA ZEMBORAIN is a poet and critic. She directs the Creative Writing in Spanish Program at NYU and is the author of several poetry collections: *Guardians of the Secret* (2009), *Mauve Sea-Orchids* (2007)

SLAVOJ ZIZEK is an associate editor of *lacanian ink*. A conspicuous lecturer and the author of a great number of writings, one of his most recent books is *Living in the End Times* (Verso, 2010).

CATHY LEBOWITZ is a writer. An editor at *Art in America*, her writing is prone to involve art and notions of Lacan. She gets published in *Art in America*, *lacanian ink*, and other media.

JOSEFINA AYERZA, member of the WAP, of the NLS, holds a private practice in NYC. She teaches at NYU. The Editor at *lacanian ink*, she writes in artists' catalogues and for L'Âne, Hurly-Burly, Du...

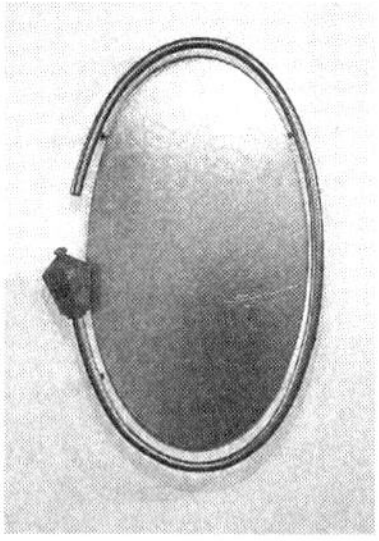

Covers:

MARTIN KIPPENBERGER

MIRROR FOR HANG-OVERBUD, 1990

Wood, metal, casting resin, aluminum foil

145 x 97 x 23 cm

TIEFES KEHLCHEN (DEEP THROAT), 1991

To resume again…

Is the couch a Symptom?

If something, the couch is the actual element around which our practice gets structured. The new thing is that the couch has stars. Why?—because we are talking America. The model comes from France, like the babies, like Pierre-Rey who continues to tell about… Not the stars. They come from the American flag, shining on the couch to greet the First Paris-USA Lacan Seminar with which we will in turn honor the 30th Anniversary of Lacan's death.

> This happened several times in the course of the performance. She would rise from the couch to dive onto the stage, then return from the stage to dive into the couch. During the intervals, I kept up my strength with caviar.
>
> I judged that this shared intimacy would result in a state of abandon such that I would be able to talk to her about money with as little coyness as she was talking to me about love. Despite her fortune, I was surprised to hear her answer that we both had some rotten luck. That very same morning she had had to pay a huge amount of back taxes which had left her bloodless. I was going to be paid back in two days. I asked her whether I could help her. She thanked me effusively, but rejected my offer, arguing that she would manage on her own.
>
> The first of my two my friends was a singer. Also very well known. His jingles are on everyone's lips. His lost-child air moved me to take charge of him when he was depressed… and he often was. Now and then I would take him to Deauville and even went so far as to place a girl into his arms. Sometimes he would call me up at three in the morning. We would

solve all the world's problems. I was fond enough of him to ask him this favor.

What was extraordinary was that he too had had to pay his *taxes* that very same morning. I hung up worrying for him. He called me half an hour later. He had just had an idea. Explaining that it was for me, he would just ask ten of our common friends for the tenth part of the amount I needed, and thus he would get me out of hot water.

I thanked him profusely, and declined his generous offer.

The second of my friends wasn't a singer. He was much older than me and blackmailed others, reigning over an empire of music halls, and was what is known in the underworld as a "justice of the peace," that is to say, a man of honor chosen by his peers to ultimately settle disputes among criminals.

I had no luck with him either: *taxes*.

He was the only one to tell me the truth. A few days before, he had lent a considerable amount of money to one of my friends, to whom he wasn't even particularly close.

Whatever their confessed or real reasons, I took these refusals as acts of treason, and swore on my life that I would never allow anyone else to wound me with such an excuse.

How did I manage that night and the following days to keep my word? If I did keep it. I've forgotten.

Without asking for my opinion, Lacan would imperturbably end every session with "See you tomorrow," sending me back, my hands sweaty with anxiety, to the grayness of rue de Lille. The following day, crushing in my pocket the money which I had managed to gather after a terrible search—for how long would I be able to pull off that daily miracle?—I would find myself again in his office.

For his own part, he was always exquisitely polite. Cigarettes. Towards five, Gloria would serve him a cup of tea and two dates on a china saucer. His tone of voice was so friendly that it wouldn't have surprised me if he had asked me to share them with him.

Besides his tea he seemed to drink in my words. It was crucial that no mistake be made concerning myself. Trying not to show off, I would, skillfully and discreetly, keep pointing out my merits, going deeper and deeper into the ridiculous land in which an ass makes more of an ass of himself than usual in order to be given oats—or in this case, to be saved by the sound of his voice.

On the third day, instead of taking me directly into his office, Gloria led me into the small library at the back, in which she left me for five minutes in the midst of other patients. I eyed them surreptitiously. Who were they? Why were they there? Didn't they know that Lacan was waiting for me?

As soon as I was in his presence he apologized for his "delay."

I apologized profusely, taking his politeness so far as to justify his reasons and ended his sentence with an "I am not responsible" which stunned me.

On the afternoon of our fifth encounter, when, as was his habit, he shook my hand after pocketing my bills, he suddenly snapped at me:

"I've decided to take you on for analysis."

I looked at him uncomprehendingly.

"I thought we had already started."

He stood up.

"See you on Monday," he said.

The Economics of *Jouissance*

JACQUES-ALAIN MILLER

translated by ASUNCIÓN ALVAREZ

THE LACANIAN COGITO

Last time I brought up what I call the Lacanian *cogito*.

It doesn't deliver an "I am" but rather—the expression appears in Lacan's text—an "enjoys him/ herself" (*se jouit*), which would name, if we wished to transform this expression into a grammatical sentence, "a one." It's a pun on letters and sounds with *Se jouit* (enjoys him/herself) and *Je suis* (I am).

(one) enjoys oneself

In Latin, to enjoy is *gaudeo*—from which it is derived—which in Classical Latin has the meaning to rejoice (*se rejouir*). Behind the term "enjoyment," *jouissance,* there is *gaudia*—joy. I have checked the etymological dictionary, which told me that the word *jouir* comes from the late Latin *gaudire*, which in Classical Latin is *gaudere*. In the transformations which took place in the 12th century, it turned into *goïr* in French, then *joïr*. The form *jouir* didn't appear until the 13th century—in the sense of to receive joyfully someone or something, to celebrate. What dominates it is thus the value of the signification of rejoicing (*réjouissance*).

Gaudeo Gaudia Gaudire Gaudere

But from the mid 12th century on, this word took on an erotic value—signaled as such by the dictionary. It's after all a mysterious thing, a miracle, a glory of the French language. Which makes Lacanians in other languages maintain, in their own accents, the term *jouissance*. English speakers, in particular, lay down their arms before *jouissance*. They believe that it's a local specialty of us curious French natives. The fact is that the English term to enjoy—which clearly has the same source and belongs to the Latin part of the English vocabulary—didn't take on the value of experiencing pleasure, particularly sexual pleasure, which it has for us. There is also a legal use of the term *jouissance*—enjoyment of a good—but besides this the word is marked by its erotic value. It seems that only in Québec can someone still say *Je jouis de quelqu'un* (I enjoy someone) and innocently mean that they take pleasure in frequenting that person.

Will the Lacanian use of the word *jouissance* mark the language? Maybe, given that it's a use that relies on sexuality, but which extends the meaning of the word to comprise the drives—through the fact that the *jouissance* of the drives is reducible, from a certain point of view, to the *jouissance* of one's own body and, in this sense, is not sexual. We turn the sexual value of *jouissance* into a trampoline from which to leap onto a generalized *jouissance* of the body.

In analytical practice, when it comes to the manifestation of this *jouissance* of the drives, there is a passage from *Je suis* to *Se jouit*; a passage from which the self is cut out and in which the subject fades. It's the acephalous value of *Se jouit* which performs the ablation of even the impersonal one.

• From "Wo Es war..." to "Se jouit"

If we think about it, the passage from *Je suis* (I am) to *Se jouit* (It enjoys him/herself) is the inverse of the passage which Freud turned into an imperative: the all-too-famous "*Wo Es war, soll Ich werden,*" translated as "Where the Id used to be, the Ego must come," which Lacan, more poetically and also in different ways, translated as "Where It used to be, I (*je*) must come to be"—*Ich* having here the meaning of the subject, *Je*.

This injunction expresses a demand for subjectivation. Where that used to be, where the acephalous and silent drive used to be—the silence of the drives which Freud famously talks about—the subject must come, the subject of the signifier. This is what is familiarly known as the final word in psychoanalysis: putting into words what remained silenced or, in an even more familiar way, what remained unsaid.

For us, putting something into words—until we eventually correct this conception—is quite mortifying. Let us stress the homophony: mo(t)rtification! (where *mot* means "word" in French). This is a conception, made classic by Lacan—to whom it doesn't really belong—by which the word is the death of the thing: the signifier, particularly the signifier which designates you—your name—will survive you. The species seeks the survival of the name. When the Pope was here in front of the *Yad Vashem*, he articulated that the names of those who disappeared will not disappear—that's easy to say. Obviously, he meant: they won't disappear because those who loved them will remember them.

On the one hand, the signifier survives—not you. On the other hand, as Lacan developed in many ways, the signifier kills. He even pointed out how death appears in the French personal pronoun *tu*, taking the value of *tuant* or *tué* ("killing" or "killed").

In this sense, subjectivisation is a negativisation.

Even if we don't take this radical point of view, there is the idea that talking about something wears it out, that it empties a libidinal reservoir which is imprisoned in silence.

But I was speaking about its exact opposite.

With Lacan, we are dealing with *Wo Ich war, soll Es werden*. "Where I (*je*) used to be, *jouissance* must come"—I don't know if that makes sense in German; no doubt it does, as it's modeled on Freud's *Wo Es war, soll Ich werden*. The point is to make *jouissance* come, to make it appear. This is what might be given as the formula for Lacanian interpretation: Where the I (*je*) used to be, *jouissance* must come.

Lacan was able to write that *jouissance* is always spoken between the lines, between the signifiers—which means that it is never properly spoken, that what can be said about it kills it. Some *jouissance* disappears.

Let us consider that *jouissance* which remains alive. In this sense, there is no *jouissance* without life. We don't know what life is any more than we know what *jouissance* is. All that we can say is that there is a sense of belonging between these two signifiers—I dare not say concepts: life, *jouissance*. If there is no *jouissance* without life, then it cannot be signified. It can be said that there is no *jouissance* without life. But can we say that there is no life without *jouissance*? We can pose the question. Do plants enjoy? In what sense do animals enjoy? If this is the case, we know nothing about it. As for speaking beings, we know about it on the basis of what they tell us when they speak. It seems difficult to withdraw *jouissance* from animal life, at least when we hear these animals. As for fish, it's obviously more mysterious, even if we can listen to them with special devices. All this indicates that, when we talk about the signifier, it's not only a matter of taking it from the—obviously important—aspect of its signification effects, but also in its materiality as a sound. Not only sense, but also sound. Not only the word, but also the cry. There is, it seems, some affinity between *jouissance* and the cry. When the cry is replaced by writing in the order of the signifier, it seems to move away from the dimension of *jouissance*. We don't have the same testimony at all in writing.

When Lacan said that *jouissance* is only spoken between the lines—which already implied that he had distinguished *jouissance* as such, at least by means of a word—he assigned to it, with respect to the order of the signifier, the same place as he assigned to desire, as he regarded desire as what was left unsaid, what could not be said about demand, the margin that every demand leaves before or behind.

• Desire and *jouissance*

Desire and *jouissance*—which amount to an effort to arrange the analytic experience along two vectors—are the two interpretations which Lacan distinguished within Freud's libido. I said this in the past, when I realized this fact. These are two interpretations which at the start shared the fact of being metonymic with regard to the signifying chain, the fact that they were in a sliding position, that they could not be captured or grasped.

Simply put, we might say that one of these two interpretations—the interpretation of libido as desire—is a negative interpretation, and that the other one—the interpretation of libido as *jouissance*—is, by contrast, positive.

The first interpretation is negative inasmuch as desire is articulated around a lack—this is Lacanianism 101. This lack is solved when it is bared. It then appears, *après coup,* after the deed, that desire was a bubble which was only, as Lacan put it, the metonymy of a lack. This is desire's lying truth. Besides, when Lacan had the idea that the experience of the pass might have a logical conclusion, he gave two formulas, the first of which, on the side of desire, ended with the matheme for castration—minus phi—as the only, and negative, substance of desire.

$$(-\phi)$$

The second interpretation, the interpretation of libido as *jouissance*, is something else entirely. Although what we have here, as I said a few weeks ago, is a plus and a minus, this minus, nonetheless, is not hereby negative. It's a minus which is a not so much, a less. Variations in *jouissance* are variations in intensity which remain in the positive.

There is—to put it in a short-circuit form—a lying truth of desire, a truth which makes us question its own point. Desire is marked by the question: What do I really desire? When it comes from the Other, this question takes the form which Lacan gave us by means of the Italian expression *Che vuoi*?—an expression which he had found in a novel by Jacques Cazotte, *The Devil in Love,* at the point in which the devil appears under the form of a disgusting camel's head, leaving behind his previous appearance as a charming little blonde, the narrator's beloved: Biondetta. The horror of this *Che vuoi* arises from within this ravishing apparition—in Italian in the original text, although the rest of the novel is in French. This might make us think of Edgar Allan Poe's novella, *The Angel of the Odd*[1]—an angel which, oddly enough, speaks in a very strong German accent. In *The Devil in Love*, it's in Italian. The narrator's desire was apparently satisfied by this charming object which then turned out to be a camel. This makes it obvious that the narrator hadn't reached the end of his desire, as he had made a stop at this peaceful oasis.

Thus there is a lying truth of desire, whereas—playing on Marshall Pétain's august formulation, "*jouissance* doesn't lie." You may remember the illustrious slogan which Pétain's speechwriter, the famous Emmanuel Berl, came up with: "The earth doesn't lie." Well, *jouissance* doesn't lie. In this sense, it isn't marked by negativity. Lacan used as a symbol—correlative to desire's minus phi—the capital Phi which cannot be negativized:

$$\Phi$$

2. The Equivocation of *objet a*

If we try to locate and gauge the usage of *objet a* in psychoanalytical practice, it's a very equivocal matheme, as it borrows from desire and *jouissance*—from minus phi (-φ) and capital Phi (Φ).

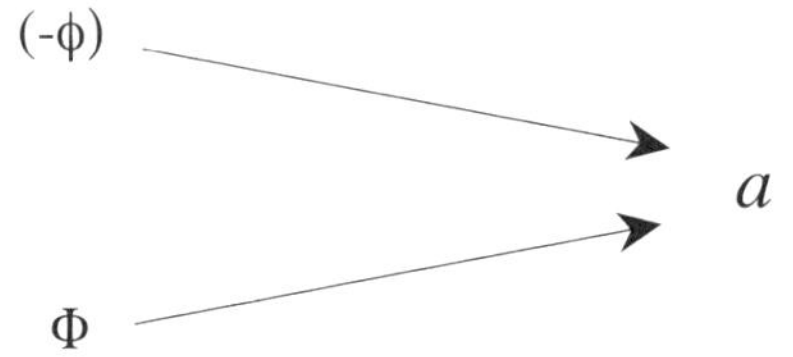

This is why its use has surpassed all other mathemes in Lacan's teaching. *objet a* is equivocal because it is essentially positive and at the same time it involves castration at its core. Let us say that *objet a* is an amboceptor between desire and *jouissance*. Nothing shows it better than the two definitions which Lacan gave of them over time. If Lacan developed this concept, which he created, to such an extent, it was because it is a term which carries out a sort of mediation between desire and *jouissance*, a mediation between the deceits of desire and the positive constancy of *jouissance*.

This mediation only lasted until the solution to the paradoxes of experience by *objet a*, that is to say, salvation by the *objet a*, appeared in Lacan as a mark of the semblant, which seemed to him to pale as regards the real. Lacan gave consistency to it by means of some extraordinary logical and topological constructions, but as regards the real, *objet a* is nonetheless a theoretical artifice. It functions as a *jouissance* unit to be used in analysis, a unit which would be the aim of interpretation and in which the analysand would find the key to his or her being.

• Assuredly Signifying

How was the *objet a* invented? As I see it, it resulted from the genius idea of transferring, of transporting or exporting the structure of language onto *jouissance*, onto the substance of *jouissance*, which appears so hard to capture. Saussure's structural linguistics provided a device, a grid, an articulation, and then *jouissance* was regarded as being ordered by it. Lacan is the proof that one can talk for a rather long time, trying to strengthen this hypothesis, to give it beauty, consistency, and credibility, until a certain breakdown takes place—namely, the fact that all this does not hold up. In any case, in Lacan's teaching, the transfer of *jouissance* onto the structure of language does not hold up. This does not mean that everything should be torn down and we should start all over, but we must realize that this enterprise is inadequate to capture the experience of the substance of *jouissance*.

This transport-export enterprise was developed by Lacan under the form: the drive is a signifying chain. Why not? Why not say, indeed, that a drive is a demand, a demand which cannot be refused—to put it like Marlon Brando in *The Godfather*, a headless demand: it's a bodily demand.

It is only on the level of drives that the English word "demand" is valid, as in English the word "demand" has the meaning of an exigency (unlike the French *demande*, which means a request). Thus, the English term is not entirely appropriate to translate the demand formulated by the speaking subject; the correct translation would be "to ask," "to ask for." When translating Lacan, "demand" would really be valid only on the level of the drives.

Lacan tells us that the drive is a signifying chain. One needs to have good will to accept this starting point! If there is no good will, we have what Lacan says: that it is a signifying chain whose elements are the fantasmatic objects: the oral object, the anal object, the phallus—"objects which are," as he says in the *Écrits* (that's how his construction started)—"assuredly signifying." When I was deciphering Lacan's teaching in the past and I came upon "The direction of the cure..."—even though I had taken this teaching at a time when Lacan had already spoken about *objet a* as being completely different from a signifier—I remember having placed a question mark next to this "assuredly signifying." "Assuredly signifying" resulted from a conception—a conception which remained crucial to Lacan—consisting in transporting the linguistic structure onto *jouissance*, in transforming the drive into a signifying chain, which involved saying that these objects were signifiers. How can you say otherwise, given that they have names? Thus this doctrine can be argued for.

What is known as Lacan's theory developed as follows: it's a series of arguments. There is—and I'm simplifying—an insight, a starting hypothesis, and then Lacan brings in the arguments which make it believable. We can even see him, from one week to another, fail to convince himself and take the argument up from another point of view. These are attempts—the attempt to transport *jouissance* onto the structure of language being a large one. This attempt was, in a way, more naïve at the start. The idea of transferring the structure of language onto *jouissance* would last for more than a decade for Lacan, but, at the start, he captured it more concisely, in a more naïve way. Hence we can see how this assuredly signifying phrase arises.

When I was looking for this passage in "The direction of the cure," I also found the passage which Victoria Wollard asked me about on Monday evening. Her question wasn't easy to answer, as she was asking me about two different English translations of a passage by Lacan, without providing the original French text—no doubt, she thought that I know all of Lacan's work by heart. I quote this passage by Lacan which appears on page 617 in the French version of the *Écrits*:

> By the intermediation of demand, all the past opens ajar until the deep end of early childhood. The subject has never done anything other than demand, he was only able to live thanks to that, and we take over.

I was asked about the translation of *nous prenons la suite* ("we take over"). There clearly was a difficulty translating the end of the sentences. And "we take over" obviously means that, as psychoanalysts, we take over inasmuch as, also in analysis, the subject continues to demand.

Lacan's distinction between demand and desire—which was particularly striking for us back in the day due to its clarity and its capacity to arrange the phenomena in the psychoanalytic experience—didn't simply have the aim of detaching the function of desire, but also the function of the drive as a higher form of demand, that is to say a demand whose elements are not the signifiers of language but the signifiers of the body. It's a higher form of demand, as Lacan's graph is built on the basis of this schema. It involves two lines, the lower line being the line of demand, and the upper line that of the drive—conceived as parallel, that is to say, simultaneous on the temporal level, in which signifiers are organic signifiers, as Lacan expressed himself at the time. The upper chain is, he says, "constituted by signifiers, that is, it develops in terms of the drive."

• The Second Treasure of Language

In the same way as we have the capital A signifier on the lower level—where the phonematic battery of language, the dictionary and all which can be gathered in an indistinct manner under the

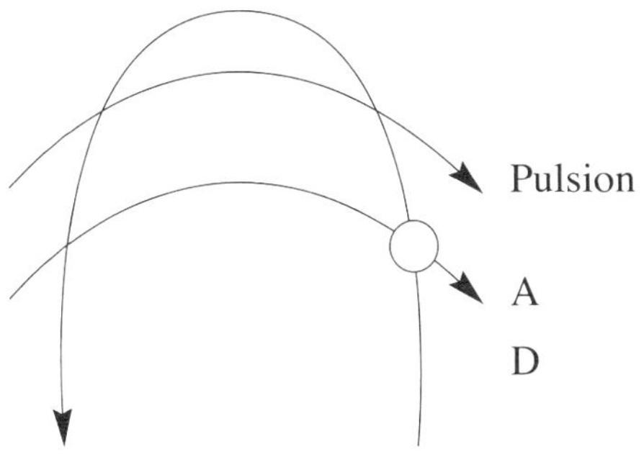

name of the treasure of language are supposed to be co-present—we have, on the higher level of the graph, a second treasure of language. You will find this in "The subversion of the subject and the dialectics of desire," as Lacan kept perfecting his approach over the years. I will call this second treasure of language, which contains the language of the body, A_2 for the time being. These are the archives of the demand of the drive, the archives of what can be called, even today, the archaic traces.

It's in this level that Lacan locates the matheme $(\$ \lozenge D)$, which I have commented on at length in the past, which designates the acephality of the demand of the drive, in which the subject manifests its disappearance by means of the bar that strikes through it, it being understood that a demand also vanishes as a demand of words, as a spoken demand.

• The Cut and the Phallus

Lacan kindly tells us that what remains is the cut itself, the cut which is found—and I'm simplifying—when it comes to *jouissance*.

Lacan thus lays the basis for the introduction of the structure of language in the *jouissance* of the cut—the cut which isolates language units, but which is found in the delimitation of erogenous zones which, in the organism, are edge zones. We have, if I may say so, a sort of embroidery of drive objects. We believe that this cut present on the level of *jouissance* is what articulates *jouissance* in the structure of language, what makes it in accordance with this structure.

This cutting word remains—which Lacan also validates by means of topology: we cut with scissors and obtain transformative effects on the structure of mathematical objects—remains equivocal. The linguistic cut actually introduces negativity, less, whereas the cut which can be designed on the libidinal level does not cancel out the positivity of the whole. The term "cut" is thus an amboceptor. It owes its popularity to its nature as such—a popularity which it has preserved in common Lacanian usages, in the various communities which refer to Lacan's work.

We have an ambiguity of desire and *jouissance*, a linguistic-libidinal ambiguity, with which we believe we can solve the paradoxes posed by the psychoanalytic experience.

What justifies my writing a second big Other, a pseudo-second big Other on the upper level of the graph, is the fact that Lacan brought together correlatively on this same graph the paradoxes of S(Ⱥ)—strictly signifying paradoxes. He pushes the signification of drives so far that it affects all the signifying paradoxes of S(Ⱥ) at the second crossing point, finding the negativity of Ⱥ and only preserving positivity through the big S which appears in the matheme—an unbarred big S which remains, whatever Lacan said afterward, the signifier which is not negativized on this level. Thus it is the equivalent of the big Phi (Φ), which cannot be negativized.

What Lacan means to preserve is the signifier for *jouissance*. He designates this signifier by means of a phallic emblem, by positing that it is the phallus that embodies *jouissance*. Saying that it is the phallus that embodies *jouissance*—as he writes—only means one thing: it isn't the body that embodies *jouissance*. This means that, in the body, *jouissance* is negativized and that what is impossible to negativize about said *jouissance* focuses on the phallus. If we take this formula, we must say that, as such, it does not hold.

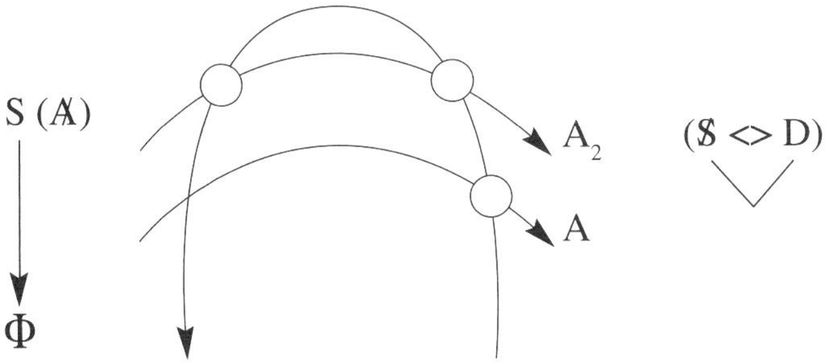

Why should the phallus, its image, its signifier, not be privileged? All evidence points in this direction. But believing that the embodiment of *jouissance* is reserved to the phallus is completely outrageous! The point of view by which it is the body that embodies *jouissance* makes much more sense. The notion of an enjoying substance, the notion that there is a status of the body as a body of *jouissance* makes much more sense! Which does not prevent, mind you, that this *jouissance* can condense in areas of the body. And all this, ultimately—and this is the reason—because Lacan, for the most part of his teaching—we can see it retrospectively—had to locate *jouissance*. One cannot handle *jouissance* unless it is located! We can follow the strands of *jouissance* throughout his teaching; we can see how he assigns various areas to it.

At first—and there is always plenty of evidence every time—he assigned *jouissance* to the phallus: Look this way! It's the phallus that embodies *jouissance*, this is the point of everything! Whether it is in the anatomy of the body, in the imaginary, or in the symbolic, the point of everything is for the phallus to embody *jouissance*.

Then he located *jouissance* in the fantasms. Given that here we have an extraordinary multiplicity, Lacan invented the fundamental fantasm. There had to be one fundamental fantasm in order for *jouissance* to be located, one single fantasm! We have here the same logic which made him locate *jouissance* in the phallus. The fact that the objects of the drives can condense *jouissance* is owed to the One phallus, they can only be thought from the phallic function. It was this same phallic logic that would give rise to the concept of the fundamental fantasm. Lacan only employed this expression once or twice in writing. And everyone then went: What is my fundamental fantasm? Everyone does well to seek it. The quest for the fundamental fantasm is a valid support for analytic research within the framework of the lying truth. But, from our point of view—a bit distant, taking one step back—what we see is how this unary—and even unian—logic, this logic of the One, imposes its shape onto Lacan's thinking.

3. From the fantasm to interpretation

What can be said about this logic? It's marked by what Lacan would later highlight as a trait proper to masculine sexuation. It was only when he approached feminine sexuation—by means of his logic, but twisting it, complicating it—that he distanced himself from this logic of the One, this unian logic.

• The fantasmatic molecule

What is the fantasm for Lacan? It's a sort of molecule, in the sense in which a molecule is a set of particles or atoms which constitute a small mass of matter. A molecule is susceptible to transformation in the course—this is what it's called—of a chemical reaction. When Lacan writes the fantasm down by means of this matheme $\$ <> a$, it's as a chemical formula, like H_2O for water, CH_4 for methane. It's a molecule whose two elements, $\$$ and *a,* are susceptible of being detached from each other.

Chemistry teaches us that molecules are rather easily transformed: we pour the right thing, we heat it, and that transform the molecules. I'm not going beyond recreational chemistry. However, atoms are much less stable. In order to transform atoms, we need what is known as a nuclear reaction. In order to transform the subject atom and the *a* atom, we must act on the nuclear level. The fundamental fantasm, as a molecule, is, this form aside, composed of a significance atom and a *jouissance* atom. This only takes place, on the level of the fundamental fantasm, at the time of the crossing of the aforementioned fantasm—and crossing here brings to mind

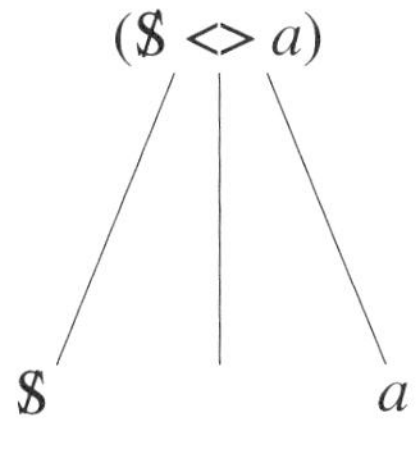

an alchemical term. Every interpretation operates on one such molecule; every interpretation is aimed at detaching the significance atom and the *jouissance* atom in the fantasmatic molecule.

It's not certain that it is right to talk as if there were a substance of *jouissance* which precedes the atom of significance and is independent from it. We can be tempted to do so. When we talk with a certain lassitude about this subject, we move in this direction—as we always do nowadays even though *objet a* is something that is lame within Lacanian theory: it is no longer at the forefront. We say: *jouissance*. By this very fact, we distinguish what is restricted and unitary about *objet a* with regard to this *jouissance*, which Lacan himself, in his Seminar *Encore*, marked with a big J surrounded by a space which designated a sort of amorphous matter.

(*a*)

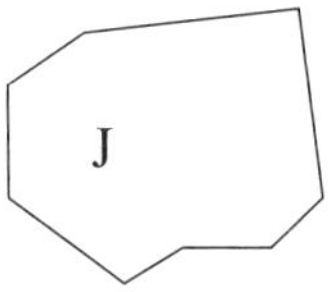

There is a tendency to talk about *jouissance* as an amorphous matter, for the very good reason that *jouissance* is taken to be the real we consider that there is no predicate that suits it. Put otherwise, we turn *jouissance* into an antepredicative, as good old Husserl put it—that is to say, something which concerns all that can be experienced and felt before the grid of predicates seizes the matter of the question.

Is there a substance of *jouissance* which precedes the signifier and is independent from it? The molecule was recalled, if things are to be temporarily arranged, in order to show that the atom of *jouissance* entails the atom of significance. What Lacan developed regarding the mark was precisely of this order: the signifying mark which mortifies *jouissance* and performs a loss is necessary for surplus *jouissance* to appear as a supplement.

Which truly makes us see that, in what Lacan called *objet a*, *jouissance* is shaped by the mold of the signifier.

• THE INTERFERENCE OF THE LYING TRUTH

If we maintain our distance with regard to this reference, the fact remains nonetheless that this construction highlights the fact that, where the appearance of *jouissance* is concerned, it always comes as a replacement, even if it no longer could be located within a unit. Even if we admit that *jouissance* is everywhere, that *jouissance* is of the body, the fact remains nonetheless that everything works as though it had been lost and found again like Eurydice—found again, but as an other—which means that it isn't the real one. Psychoanalysis would have no consistency if the analytic experience weren't run through by the thread by which the existing *jouissance* is the one that shouldn't be there.

It's on this level that negativity is introduced. Negativity is not introduced on the Se *jouit* level. It is introduced on the level in which it enjoys itself, but where it shouldn't be enjoying itself like that. There is an interference of the lying truth in *jouissance* which does not lie.

What about the signifier at work? It's because we cannot be sure that there is *jouissance* where there is no signifier that we must suppose that the signifier doesn't only have effects regarding the signified, but also effects regarding *jouissance*. This would be comparable to bells. If the first time a bell peals a crack appears, every time the bell is played, you will still hear this crack in the bell. *Jouissance* is this crack, it's the crack in the bell.

• A MODE OF SAYING

If interpretation is measured by *jouissance*, then interpretation is requested, not because of its sense effects, but because of its *jouissance* effects. It not only concerns us because of its effects regarding the signified, but also because of its embodied effects. This is what led Lacan to think about a real sense effect.

If interpretation is measured by *jouissance*, we are forced to elaborate interpretation as a special mode of saying, which does not belong to the dimension of signification or to the dimension of truth, but which emphasizes materiality, sound, in the signifier. This is the hypothesis which Lacan arrived at—and it's a radical hypothesis.

We have indeed started out from afar. It's not clear whether Freud at first made a difference between interpretation and construction. It was only at the end of his career that he isolated the construction of knowledge, saying that it is distinct from what the analysand should be told. But the concept of interpretation nonetheless comes from here, from the communication of knowledge. The very moment interpretation is measured by the existence of *jouissance*, the interpretation of knowledge has migrated toward the cry. That's why Lacan was able to say that maybe effective interpretation was related to ejaculation, that is to say, to a use of the signifier which has no signification purpose, no purpose pertaining to the signified, but in which it is the sound, the very consistency of the sound, which might ring the bell of *jouissance* in a suitable way, in order to be satisfied.

Here we are forced to establish a disjunction between *jouissance* and satisfaction. There would be no analytic experience if *jouissance* were satisfactory. It is precisely because the worm is inside the very fruit of *jouissance* that an analysis is conceivable in which an ejaculation can rectify—as Lacan put it early on when he spoke about subjective rectification as the first moment of the analysis—rectify not the subject, but *jouissance*. This would be a justification of *jouissance*, so that it can be conceived as satisfactory.

I have touched upon—or at least referred to—this target which is the economics of *jouissance*.

Lacan was able to say—it's in his Seminar *Encore*—at the time when he took the turn of his last teaching, that it was not yet at the end of our fingertips, and that nonetheless there would be a small interest in that happening.

Even though I have abundantly glossed the years prior to

this last teaching, I could adopt the formula of the economics of *jouissance* in order to provide the gist.

This is not an invitation to become thrifty, but rather to try and clarify the distribution of this *jouissance*: its distribution in the symptom and in the fantasm, its distribution in the word and in the body.

The word "economics" has a purely Freudian origin. Freud used the term economics to refer to the point of view to be taken regarding libido—its circulation, its organization—which should be distinguished from the topographical distribution of the unconscious, the subconscious, and the conscious. The economic point of view, given by Freud when he was engaged in the elaboration of psychoanalysis, was already distinct from the wonders which appeared before him from interpretation as a deciphering.

Deciphering was Lacan's starting point. He had given its foundation in the "structure of language"—between inverted commas—taken from structural linguistics—a loan which followed on the footsteps of Lévi-Strauss, who had himself been taught by Roman Jakobson. Lacan brought a number of modifications to this structure of language, so that it could be of use to psychoanalysis, so that it could serve it. It was a matter of signifiers, of signifying elements, of signification effects, and of the relationship between signifier and signified. Lacan had added to his pot the theory of communication, which was a matter of speaker and recipient, of message, of reading and punctuation.

The economics of *jouissance* is something else altogether.

After twenty years' worth of constructions, Lacan was able to say that it still wasn't within his grasp. Is it any more within our grasp now—we who followed him in his last effort, in this turning which consists in trying to give this economics of *jouissance* an articulation which might prevail with regard to the structure of language?

4. The enjoying substance

What is at least within our grasp is apparently something which I will today call, to amuse myself, the philosophy of *jouissance*, for, when it comes to *jouissance*, we had already used, these last times, the term "substance." I had even added the term "ante-predicate," which had occurred to me—ante in the sense of before. The ante-predicate designates what is beyond predication—not as in religious preaching (*prédication* means both "predication" and "preaching" in French), but predication in the sense of the logic of the predicate. It I wanted to keep it brief, I'd say that the ante-predicate is that whereof one cannot speak, what can only be experienced.

It is rare for us to use the word "substance," as it was for Lacan, from whom it comes nonetheless. When we introduced it, we didn't say that *jouissance* was a substance. We only said that, inasmuch as we might come to grasp the concept of *jouissance*—as implied by the word "concept"—evoked the concept of substance, a reference to substance is required. Our interest focused on the expression enjoying substance. In this expression, it is *jouissance*, enjoyment itself that is a predicate. We have introduced a substance which enjoys, and given that we only designate this substance by means of this fact, we could say, using Descartes's term, that this *jouissance* would be the principal attribute of the aforementioned substance.

• Descartes and Aristotle

It is actually in Descartes that this curious adjunction of *jouissance* to the game of substances is rooted and motivated. Descartes distinguished between two substances: the thinking substance and the extended substance—bodies, particularly living bodies, which we need in our enjoying substance, being resorbed, like its modes in the extended substance.

If we take as our starting point Cartesian substance dualism, psychoanalysis involves providing other modifications to it.

The conception that we can have, with Descartes, of thinking substance, is obviously modified by the appearance, the discovery and need to locate what Freud called the unconscious—which is made of thoughts. The subject which we deal with in the analytic experience doesn't come from the *cogito*, doesn't come from the thinking subject. The existence of the subject in psychoanalysis comes from the speaking subject. In psychoanalysis, thinking and speaking are two different things.

In an analytic session, the thinking subject shuts up! I came across this yesterday with a patient: Yes?... Yes?—I said—and this is an entire speech when said in the adequate tone, which is deciphered as So, is it coming up? This subject, under the guise of a patient, came to see me in the form of I have too many ideas. This is a point where we can verify the disjunction between the thinking subject and the speaking subject.

There's no harm in the subject's thinking at full tilt between sessions, but, in the analytic session, the device involves the subject's sacrificing—one hopes—the abundance of his thought to the fact of thinking, to the fact of speaking a lot in the time left for him to do so. It's from therc that we hope that a certain "I am" which is not too evanescent will take form, consistency, weight. If we locate ourselves in the thread of consequences of what is said, we expect to attain, as Lacan says, "a certain real." If there is a sum, its total made up throughout experience, it's on the basis of what is spoken, not on the basis of what is thought. In consequence, we understand that Lacan was able to appropriate communication schemas and that we continued to follow him along this path.

However, the speaking subject is not at all a substance. The psychoanalytical hypothesis is rather that it is the unconscious that actually makes the substances—besides, Freud himself tried to naturalize it, so the fans of the neurosciences say. What we call subject in psychoanalysis is not a substance; it's only a premise. It resembles a substance because, in the imaginary, it is placed beneath phenomena, beneath what appears. But the subject as the subject of the signifier, once speech has reduced to the signifying chain, is what is supposed of the articulation of a couple of signifiers—nothing else. It's even the value that can be given to the familiar sign $\$$—subject is not substance.

$\$$

Aristotle sharply distinguished, in his categories, the term *ousia*, which, under a Latinized form, yielded our substance, and the term *hypokeimenon*, which Lacan regarded as the counterpart of what he called the subject—the confusion between both terms being particularly regrettable. The entire structure of language such as we make use of it is actually elaborated in the element of the non-substantial. When we talk about the signifying articulation, we mean that a signifier is not a substance which can be conceived in itself, but rather is relative to another signifier, namely to the set of signifiers. The structuralist point of view, as such, is closely linked to the non-substantial.

I was saying that I would start to give a philosophy of *jouissance*, but I am only sketching it out, as I take into account both your knowledge and your interests. Let us bear in mind at least that in *jouissance* we are dealing with a certain modification of the thinking substance. Correlatively, the enjoying substance is also a conceptual modification of the extended substance in that it reintroduces the body into it, the unity of the living body.

When we risk the expression enjoying substance, we are dealing with bodily substance. We are dealing with the living body regarded as a substance, whose main attribute would be *jouissance* as an affection of this body. *Jouissance* would be the property and the affection of the living body. I don't think it's going too far to say that the enjoying substance works as the essential attribute, in the sense in which Descartes understood it, as Lacan says that the only thing that can be known about it is that it is what enjoys itself.

Obviously, Lacan did not always stick to the rigor of this position about *jouissance* as the self-affection of the living body. For a long time, following the *Encore* seminar and in his last teaching, he tested out a sort of intersubjectivity of *jouissance*, involving the Other in the economics of this *jouissance*: that's the *jouissance* of the body of the Other. Thus he tried to insinuate a sort of dialectical process into *jouissance*, but this elaboration nonetheless ended with the fact that there is no *jouissance* of the Other, that it is essentially imaginary and not at all in the same order as the *jouissance* of one's own body.

It may well be that the *jouissance* of one's own body turns your body into something alien with regard to yourself, that this body that is yours becomes an Other. There are modalities of this strangeness: I can no longer feel my body, or I imagine another body which *jouis* instead of mine, I can only *jouït* it when I imagine that there's someone else's body in my place in the sexual relationship. In this regard, the figure of the Other insinuates itself into *jouissance*, but it's nonetheless of a different order than the experience which some people have when they feel as though they were hovering over their own bodies.

This is more in the line of the elementary phenomena found in psychosis. It's all a matter, not only of the text, but also of the stress placed. The dimension of having a body, the full certainty that it's your own body, the massive, bold yes to one's own body, is not up to everyone. *Jouissance* is doubtlessly a property of the body which is lent to and seized by the Other, but what I am designating is something else: namely that, in its deepest aspect, *jouissance* is a self-affection of the living body—which does not exclude the fact that its cause—or trigger—may be external to this bodily substance.

• Heidegger and Husserl

In this philosophy of *jouissance*, one cannot but wonder about the antepredicative status of *jouissance*. All the less so in that the current usage of this word, as far as I've been able to hear or read it, *jouissance* is readily classified under this category.

The fact that *jouissance* is antepredicative means, to simplify, that nothing of what can be said about it is inadequate. *Jouissance* would thus belong to what Husserl—the founder of phenomenology, a philosopher who is passionately deciphered and who has occupied a large part of the best minds of the 20th century, the teacher of Heidegger, who was his university assistant—designated as the *Lebenswelt*: the life world. In order to develop this concept, I would need an amount of time that I lack, given that the word "world" itself is a coded one in Husserl's language. We go from there to what Heidegger called, in *Being and Time*, being-in-the-world. I can only give a brief sketch of it here. I will say that the life world would be the ideal of isolating, or at least designating, a radical level of experience. This would be Heraclitus's flux, the flux of elementary experience, or rather the original flux beyond all form of discourse. The flux which would remain always underneath discourse, underneath all that is informed by it, underneath all which is shaped by discourse, including forms on the perceptual level. Through this flux, the life world would escape all predication. If it's an affirmation, it's an affirmation beyond yes and no, beyond true and false. Let us say that it's a true which has no opposite. In this sense, it is doubtlessly not too much to formulate that this *Lebenswelt* cannot be said but only experienced. Hence its status as being's first experience.

This is obviously not saying too much about the *Lebenswelt*. I will not judge whether this is fully orthodox from a Husserlian point of view. Back when I was studying philosophy, I was very careful before I would say anything about Husserl. There were some extremely vicious watchdogs who had access to Husserl's last manuscripts, which had accumulated at the University of Louvain, in the hands of very scrupulous priests who would only open their doors to selected scholars. It was Husserl himself who was antepredicative: you can say nothing about him without being contradicted. Did this drive me away from him? Maybe. What I am trying to transmit here is a *Lebenswelt* which Lacanians can use.

As I see it, *Lebenswelt* has an absolute status. It's an absolute of the infra order. In order to approach it, one must take an apophatic way—not apophantic but apophatic; one letter makes a huge difference—that is to say, a negative way, as in negative theology in which you can only say what God isn't, not what He is. Lacan's real is akin to the *Lebenswelt* in certain of its traits, in that the *Lebenswelt* involves an apophatic way. In any case, the apophatic way towards the real is something that is very stressed upon in Lacan's teaching: when you say what it is, it's somewhere else.

What remains, in this limit-concept of the *Lebenswelt*, is that life is necessary—life, which remains an *x*. No *jouissance* without life, without a life carried by a body, an organism, namely a cell. There are plenty of imaginings of *jouissance* without life or after life, namely the idea of the afterlife—maybe characterized by what is hardly ever found in the first life: bliss. There is also an imagining of the *jouissance* of the living dead, which would lend itself to a vast anthropological research, a *jouissance* which mankind unanimously believes wishes us no good. But despite the bliss of souls and the appetite of vampires, there is no *jouissance* without life.

If we turn the saying around, if we say "no life without *jouissance*," then we must say that there is no doubt an antepredicative status of *jouissance* which can and must be inferred of *jouissance* wherever there is life. Lacan even made apologues wondering about the *jouissance* of plants or of the lilies of the field. At that point, he was obviously dealing with a status of *jouissance* which included pleasure, with the certain characteristic that nobody says anything about it. But if we don't want to become delusional—which would be amusing, but that is not my aim—we should go back to asking how and under what form we find this *jouissance* in psychoanalysis. We must ask ourselves how this *jouissance* figures in it.

Before that, I would like to distinguish the subject's $\$$ and the big, unbarred S of substance

S

• Spinoza

It was Spinoza who gave a modern, brief, well thought out definition of substance. It is worth remembering. It appears in Book 1 of the *Ethics* as Definition III: By substance I understand what is in itself and conceived by itself: that is to say, that whose concept does not require the concept of something else from which it should be formed. This definition has a superb self-sufficiency. It's a definition of substance given to allow Spinoza, after some strikes or some movements of his pieces on the board against the invisible adversary against whom he was playing, in his game against the Other whom he tried to convince and checkmate—for that is what Spinoza's *Ethics* is: a perpetual checkmate against the reader—to prove that there is one single substance. Not two, as Descartes would have it, but only one, which he named God. Thus he invented a God which had nothing to do with what had been known before him. There are some slight resemblances which have been sought in Kabala, but it's nonetheless a God which is mostly known by the signifier that Spinoza gave him, as he can be said to have shown throughout the *Ethics*—in the sense in which I'm going—of what might be called a high autism.

The subject, itself—far from its concept demanding the concept of something else to be formed, far from being in itself and conceived by itself—depends on the signifier. What we call the subject depends on speech, reduced to its signifying frame. We even consider that the subject can change depending on the signifier. The concept of interpretation, the idea that the analyst's interpretation can modify the subject, implies that the subject is not a substance.

By contrast, life, the reproduction of life, does not

depend, in its concept, on the signifier. It depends—to take up here Weismann's famous dichotomy—on the transmission of the germ through the bodily generations. Only, even if we doubtlessly know what life is in the human species more than in any other species, we nonetheless have, particularly thanks to psychoanalysis, some idea about the reproduction of life. We have particularly the idea that it doesn't work on its own. Concerning life, we have the idea that its reproduction in the human species is curiously conditioned by language, by the signifier. It is not marked by any automaticity—as is proven by the refusal of reproduction, be it conscious or unconscious. To the extent that Lacan was able to say that, in the human species, the letter is analogous to the germ, that in order for the germ to be transmitted through the generations, a certain type of signifier—which Lacan called the letter in order to stress the materiality of this signifier—must be transmitted.

In the same way, if *jouissance* has an antepredicative status—which is hard to deny—it nonetheless does not seem to be antesignifying in the human species. It was from this point of view that Lacan was able to say—once—that the signifier was the cause of *jouissance*, exactly in the same way in which he was able to say that the signifier was the cause of the subject; which should nonetheless be distinguished: the signifier being the cause of the subject in discourse, where it would be the cause of *jouissance* in the body.

Even if there is a *jouissance* that is equipollent to life, even if all life involves *jouissance*, an Other *jouissance* is nonetheless specified in the human species, by the fact of the incidence of the signifier.

To brutalize things a bit, to dissipate certain poetic effects on which Lacan punned, I can provide a stratification and distinguish between the antepredicative *jouissance* of every living body and *jouissance bis*, which is the *jouissance* that becomes consistent and fixed following the incidence of the signifier, as a result of the fact that there is speech. There is not only the life world, there is also the speech world—*Sprachwelt*.

5. *Jouissance* in the Analytic Experience

It is this *jouissance bis* which we deal with in the analytic experience. We are dealing with a traumatized *jouissance*. It is not a raw *jouissance*, it's rather a brutalized *jouissance*. We arc dcaling with a displaced *jouissance*. What we are told about as analysts, what we must signify, is a *jouissance* which is presented as what shouldn't be, what is called—as Lacan called it—a *Non decet*: it's not suitable We can even say, given that the word belongs in the same etymological thread, that it's not decent.

That's why the confession of this *jouissance* always meets obstacles, as a rule. We could not write the chapter on the confession of *jouissance* in psychoanalysis without listing everything that is an obstacle to it. As for the fantasm, Freud pointed it out: one must be able to expect the patient to confess the fantasmatic imaginary scenarios which are necessary to his or her enjoyment—which is not, certainly, the fundamental fantasm, but the fantasm as an instrument, as a means to enjoy. For cxample, I collected a subject's confession (a confession which came out torturedly), trying to negotiate with, let us say, his moral conscience, with an infernal gag, in order for him to give me something which he had tried to spare me—which only made me say "but that's very mushy!", whereas he gasped at the horror and the transgression of his fantasm. This is where we can measure that this *jouissance*, whatever it may be, is not decent, from the very fact of being *jouissance*.

It is not decent, and nonetheless it must be said that not much is really invented on this level. All the horrors that you do have already been done. There are some which are punishable by law, that's a fact, but you'll notice that those are the ones that are most easily spoken about. Obviously, when a subject has no decency at all, it's an entirely different thing. There is such a thing, but after all, as a rule, decency is there.

• Fixation

In the analytic experience, *jouissance* appears above all through the bias of fixation. Otherwise, it's just little pleasures. *Jouissance* is truly recognized in fixation, that is to say, one always returns to it. The question is to know whether this "one always returns to it" is halted or not by the crossing of the fantasm.

I had mentioned that there was an aftermath to the crossing of the fundamental fantasm. There is an analytic space for the interrogation and the elaboration which opens up after the crossing of the fundamental fantasm. Maybe it is there that "I always return here" appears, maybe through other ways, eventually through more corporeal ways. It is as such that *jouissance* is next, next to what should be, as Lacan said. As such it is on the side, but we fully return to it. *Jouissance* never lies, I was saying, whereas everything else lies, is of the register of the lying truth. Whereas swelling desire, in analytic experience, is made to be thinned and deflated, *jouissance* does not lie. It does not lie inasmuch as it is in itself a misunderstanding with respect to what should be.

In order to ensure that we do not confuse *jouissance* with the real and do not turn it into an antepredicative of the analytic experience, I will take a formula from Seminar XX *Encore*. The more I try to help you to push aside Lacan's formulations that are attempts or tries which he later rejected, the more I use this formula, until further notice—I mean, until I give myself further notice—as a bookmark: Language is a device for *jouissance*.

• Cutting

What Lacan tells us is that in the human species *jouissance* uses language as a device. This is not the case in animals. Although animals can be run through by language effects, these are but parody effects, as Lacan puts it.

I am taking another formula, which is not in the *Encore* Seminar—a Seminar, besides, which was semi-improvised: Lacan only had a few formulas written in his papers. This second formula appears in the text, *Or worse*, which deals with the previous seminar, but which Lacan has drafted at the end of Seminar XX. It is found in *Autres Écrits*, page 550: Knowledge, in Lacan's usage at the time. Knowledge as a signifying articulation, affects the body of the speaking being—this is my abridgement—by fragmenting its *jouissance*, by cutting it up until it produces the failures which I turn into the *objet a*. The signifier affects the body of the *parlêtre*, the speaking being, in that it fragments the bodily *jouissance*; these fragments are the *objets a*. If we look closely at this formula, it entails that there is a first status of *jouissance*—what I called *jouissance* of life, the antepredicative *jouissance*—but which, given that the body in the human species speaks, its *jouissance* is modified under the guise of a fragmentation, of a condensation of Freud's erogenous areas, each one relative to a certain type of object—thus, fragmentation and condensation.

This is not an economics of *jouissance*, but we are as close as possible to the point reached by Lacan before his last teaching. This is the limit where we can still apply and transfer the structural linguistics grid to the economics of *jouissance*.

The linguistic grid teaches that the signifier has meaning effects. The sounds which I make bear a signification—more or less vague, a cloud, certainly, but a signification; they are not regarded as barks, as howls. Transferring this grid to the economics of *jouissance* consists in saying that the signifier also has *jouissance* effects. It is not the case that there are only meaning effects, there are also *jouissance* effects. Inasmuch as the *jouissance* effect is more consistent than the meaning effect—which is evanescent—we could say that it's a product. Rather than saying effect, we shall talk about a product. When Lacan invented his four discourses, he placed *objet a* on the level of a product inasmuch as it was symmetrical to the meaning effect. In the same way as I was able to take up the fantasmatic molecule, I can write the conjunction of the signifier or of meaning with *objet a*.

$$(s <> a)$$

This is what Lacan, a few years later, called the *jouis-sens* or the *sens-joui*—punning on the word *jouissance*. Saying *sens-joui* amounts to surmounting the binarism of meaning and *jouissance*. The more Lacan made the fantasm work as a molecule capable of being exploded into two atoms, $\$$ and *a*, the more the neologisms *jouis-sens* and *sens-joui* take the shape of an atom and not of a molecule. This is what Lacan doubtlessly tried to say when he spoke about the enjoying speech, particularly in order to qualify the analyzing speech. What this term conveys is an effort to move beyond the binarism ultimately inherited from Descartes, in which we have the signifier on one side and *jouissance* on the other.

• Two, One and three

For Lacan, there is clearly a push-toward-unarism, the search—even through puns—of saying at the same time the signifier and *jouissance*, meaning and *objet a*. Along this line, I will even go so far as to think that, if his entire last teaching appears as threefold, as based on the trinity of the real, the symbolic and the imaginary—a trinity which he had exposed a long time before, but which had never been thematized as such and brought to the forefront of his manipulations—it was ultimately to provide a device for the push-toward-unarism. The entire vector of his teaching leads to a narrow conjunction, toward a coalescence between signifier and *jouissance*, but the passage to this unarism is given a threefold character. By this push-toward-unarism, Lacan plunges into triplicity.

Lacan's teaching was, at first, dominated by two: on the one hand, by the signifying articulation and, on the other hand, by the drive, with the question of knowing how to methodically settle what is of the order of *jouissance* and drive on the basis of the signifying articulation. By the pressure of the analytic experience itself, Lacan was then led to the effort of surmounting this duality.

Finally, he surmounted this duality, not by elaborating on the one as such, but by elaborating on a three under the guise of the famous Borromean knot.

What really matters, what runs through Lacan's entire last teaching despite its triplicity—at least in my opinion and as I see it—is the search for a unitary language and an identical expression for the registers of the signifier and of *jouissance*. This is also why his entire last teaching creates an entire space of demonstrations and configurations which are precisely beyond discourse. Lacan makes room for what does not allow itself to be reabsorbed into discourse and which can only be manipulated and looked at.

The nodal structures which Lacan multiplied as he wished in his entire last teaching follow this singular idea—already expressed once in Seminar *Encore*—by which the structure is of the very text of *jouissance*. This is a paradoxal formula which appends the text to *jouissance* in order to qualify the structure. By this word, we must understand the nodal texture, which is at the same time a structure and *jouissance*. Lacan's knots are knots of *sens-joui*. It is this unit that lies at the heart of the triplicity placed at the forefront of this entire last teaching. There are three dimensions, there are three threads of string; three thus seems to dominate this reflection, whereas its invisible foundation is the one of the coalescence of the *sens-joui*.

The signifier itself is altered by this. When Lacan shows *lalangue* as the foundation of language, when he isolates it beneath the artificial constructions of language, he distinguishes in the same way the signifier from the letter—which means that, in both cases, he moves along the lines of what I will call, for lack of a better word, materiality—as is evidenced by the handling of the Borromean knots.

It is there that the interpretation that faces what lies beyond the fantasm, beyond the exploded molecule of the fantasm, which faces the atom of the *sens-joui*, becomes an ejaculation and has to do with the enjoying substance. It only attains this target by giving up the facilities of deciphering under the Father's aegis. We can only access this by shaking off, as I am doing here, the discourse of he who still appears as the second Father of psychoanalysis.

6. *Jouissance*: transgression or substitution?

As I am approaching it from the point of view of Lacan's last teaching, *jouissance* is not a transgression—unlike what is expounded in *The Ethics of Psychoanalysis*, which constitutes its pivoting point.

Jouissance, on the contrary, is a normal functioning—nothing bizarre or exceptional.

• The transgressive model

Lacan is multiple. He is not-all, I daresay. There is certainly a teaching by Lacan, among other teachings by Lacan, which expounds the concept of *jouissance* on the basis of the concept of pleasure. The concept of pleasure which it takes as its starting point is Aristotelian—a concept which has conditioned the theory of pleasure throughout the ages, which turns said pleasure into the name of a state of wellbeing.

This wellbeing is found nowadays integrated in the definition of health given by the WHO—the World Health Organization which seeks to protect us, for example, from the pandemics which the current stage of civilization facilitates by the development of the transport industry. This industry is so essential that, when a little symptom appears, when an airplane goes splash in the middle of the Atlantic, it becomes news all over the world. A progressive unification of mankind on its way to becoming One—One-all—is thus made manifest. It is so attached to its wellbeing that the wellbeing of each one appears to be the condition for the wellbeing of all.

If we take as our reference the state of wellbeing and the adjustments in functional values which it involves—which I have already represented in my course as a loop symbolizing the homeostatic regulation of the pleasure principle, which has always been attached to a midpoint: neither too much nor too little, just what is needed—*jouissance* then appears as a transgression, with a connotation of more, a supplementary value resulting from a forcing where the more turns easily into too much. Surplus pleasure thus communicates with the start of suffering—for example, with the equivocation of cries, which, in the speaking being, can spell out this irruption.

You can easily find how Lacan expounded this functioning in chapter 5 of Seminar XI, *The Four Fundamental Concepts of Psychoanalysis*, in which the regulation of pleasure is termed homeostasis, a term promoted in 1920 by physiologist Cannon, who introduced the concept. This is congruent with what Freud was able to deduce from the relief of the areas known as erogenous in the human body, the places of choice of libido from which the vector of this *jouissance* moves, transgressing the pleasure principle. When Lacan, in an analogy with Marx's economic theory, termed *objet a*, which condenses *jouissance*, as surplus *jouissance*, he was coherent, in creating this neologism, with what I will here call a model.

This model of *jouissance*—simple, solid, structuring and powerful for arranging phenomena—is actually conceived on the model of desire. It is a copy of the model of desire—which is all the better understood given that desire and *jouissance* are, for Lacan, the two terms comprised by Freud's concept of libido.

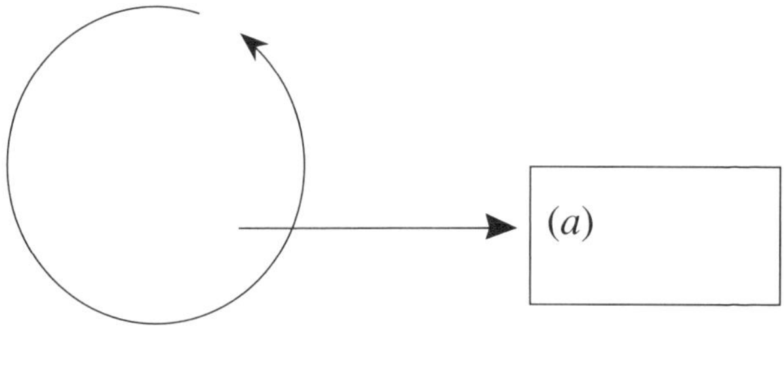

What is then this model of desire, which I am saying serves as a reference for the model of *jouissance*?

It is expounded in most detail in Seminar VII, *The Ethics of Psychoanalysis*, when Lacan surprises his audience by quoting, before giving the name of its author, a letter by Saint Paul which outlines how what is desirable depends on what is forbidden:

> I desire what is forbidden.
> I know that something is desirable because the law forbids it.
> Before the law existed, nothing was desirable.

Desire is here the effect, or rather the counter-effect, of the law. Hence the provocative formula given by Lacan, by which The law is desire—equivalence and reversibility of the law and of desire.

In this model of *jouissance*, the pleasure principle thus has the same function as the law of desire. The notion of *jouissance* as transgression transposes the relationship of desire to what is forbidden.

But *jouissance* doesn't work like that!

• *Jouissance* is not antepredicative

Jouissance does not follow the logic of desire. As far as *jouissance* is concerned, the law is inoperative. We can distinguish between forbidden, cancelled, inhibited desire and the desire that is fulfilled, that is realized—but *jouissance* falls on both sides.

Could desire be regarded as forbidden if there was not a *jouissance* of the forbidden desire? This is what is proven by what is known as ascesis—the disciplines that teach you to master desire. Isn't it blindingly obvious that there is a *jouissance* that is included in the mastery of desires? This is what is essential to what is known as ancient philosophy. A scholar, Pierre Hadot, said, very rightly, that these philosophies were constituted of spiritual exercises, of discourses that were meant to lead to a work upon oneself in order to obtain a subjective transformation, a state of happiness, a state of harmony. There was, summing up, hard work meant to obtain the regulation of desire.

This, moreover, leads us to think that talking about philosophy as a single entity is an amphibiology, a construction. In the Middle Ages, philosophy was not a spiritual exercise: it was busy compromising, trying to make agreements with theology. In modern times, the problem for philosophy was science, trying to make it fit in with the existential experience. After that, it has been finally captured by the university.

We find bits of a spiritual exercise both in what Descartes called his *Meditations* and in Spinoza's major work, the *Ethics*. The point was to achieve control over psychic life by paying attention to the event of thought, in order to acquire good habits through learning. The spiritual exercise was above all an exercise in mastery, mastery over oneself, which could only be sustained because this exercise engendered a master's *jouissance*.

This is a way of becoming aware of how *jouissance* has no opposite. If it is coordinated with a symbol, this symbol is impossible to negativize—in particular, by means of a ban. *Jouissance* is not thought of from the point of view of the law, even the positive law. The law of existing legislations regulates the distribution of enjoyment: what we have to enjoy, in what way, to which extent, etc. But this does not deal with *jouissance* as we see it: the *jouissance* of the unconscious, on an unconscious level.

Thus I remove transgression and the law from the doctrine of *jouissance*. Does this mean that I remove it from the signifier? Are the law or the rule the only figures by which the signifier is represented? I have said that, in my opinion, *jouissance* is not of the order of the antepredicative, using a term which I have taken from the philosopher, Husserl. Let us say, in Lacanian terms, that *jouissance*, the non-transgressive *jouissance* which I am thinking of, does not come before the signifier.

Jouissance is not prior to the signifier, even if it is of the body. In what we no longer call the subject but the *parlêtre*, the speaking being—as we regard it as essentially concerned by *jouissance*—the body itself, its body, does not come before the signifier either. It is not a reality prior to the signifier. By this fact, the *parlêtre* is not its body. It has its body—in the same way as someone has a good, a property, an object, which is well or badly treated, disdained, abandoned or pampered. The care that is given or not to the body denotes the unconscious value that is attributed to it.

By a sort of short-circuit, Wilhelm Reich, the crazy psychoanalyst, but sly and intelligent, thought that something essential to the practice of psychoanalysis was to observe what the patient does with his or her body. Obviously, this led him to extravagant actions which made him leave the domain of psychoanalysis. He thought he could operate directly upon the libido and upon the body and built libido "accumulators." His colleagues said no, but, truth be said, he was a realist regarding *objet a*—this object which Lacan defined as a *jouissance* condenser. Wilhelm Reich thought that *jouissance*, given its essential status, was disconnected from the signifier, that it could be treated as a kind of matter, susceptible of a physics, that it could be manipulated, captured and redistributed by means of concrete, material devices.

Everybody feels that psychoanalysis does not lead us there and that, if *jouissance* is bodily, it is nonetheless supported by language. That said, this has nothing to do with its alleged relation to the law. Language is not the law, it's an articulation.

The question is expressed in the formula which I propose: how are the body and language conjoined to produce enjoyment? I can give an answer which is not really one—for it is based on a concept of Lacan's which has its own complexity, even if you use it, if only because of the courses that I have devoted to it: In order to produce *jouissance*, body and language are conjoined in the *sinthome*.

The *sinthome* carries the body, but the *sinthome* is an articulation. Actually, we speak of the *sinthome* because there is no direct approach to *jouissance*, for this brute, imaginary *jouissance* is always refracted by the *sinthome*.

7. *Jouissance* refracted by the *sinthome*

There is a reason why Lacan chose the term *sinthome* to qualify the relation to *jouissance*—a modification, justified by etymology, of the word symptom. Symptom is a term in Freud's vocabulary which means many things. However, from the various senses which it can take in Freud's work, I will be isolating the symptom as a substitution.

• Freudian libido and masculine logic

I have reread the eighteenth lecture in the *Introduction to Psychoanalysis*—a lecture on the fixation to trauma and to the unconscious. Freud expounds that the formation of symptoms is the replacement for something else which didn't take place. This substitution value persists in the echo of Lacan's term *sinthome*.

For Freud—who read symptoms as he read dreams, slips of the tongue and jokes, the replacement in question is a linguistic replacement: the text of the symptom replaces an original text which must be replaced. There have been psychic processes which have been inhibited, concealed, there has been an interrupted message which has not reached consciousness, which has been forced to remain unconscious, and this is—both in symptoms and in dreams—what is deciphered in analysis. Freud paid homage to his colleague Breuer, who posited that symptoms disappear when their unconscious preconditions are made conscious. On this basis, he expounded to his audience that symptoms pass, disappear, once their sense is known.

This is only one of the two sides of the symptom. According to the first one, the symptom is a substitution text, but, as Freud clearly expounds, there is another, supplementary side, namely that symptoms serve sexual satisfaction: A symptom is a replacement for the sexual satisfaction which the patient is deprived of in his or her life. Thus the question is to understand symptoms as a satisfaction that replaces that which is lacking in life. Put otherwise, the symptom in neurosis is a substitutive sexual satisfaction (*satisfaction sexualle substitutive*)—please note that the initials of these three words, in French, are the same as those of the expression subject supposed to know (*sujet supposé savoir*).

S s S

• Perversion as a reference

All this is present, all these echoes are present, in the Lacanian term *sinthome*. At first, Freud illustrated this by means of perversions. He plunged into the catalog of perversions. There we see that the patient, far from being satisfied with enjoying a body of the opposite sex, enjoys certain parts of this body or parts in contact with this body, such as clothes. We see the patient move through complex scenarios and actions, far from normal coition. By means of these objects, these actions, these subjects derive a satisfaction which replaces normal sexual satisfaction.

The passage through perversion, understood as distinct from neuroses, enabled Freud to show that the same substitution process is at work in neurosis—most notably, in hysteria. The hysterical subject can attach his symptoms to all the organs in the body, for example in the hysterical paralyses and hypersthesias which are so many substitutive sexual satisfactions. If Freud took perversion as a reference, it was to show that substitutive *jouissance* is also present in neurosis and that it is capable of disturbing bodily functions. As he says: Organs behave as substitutive genital organs.

What better way to mark the affinity between substitutive *jouissance* and the signifier than to say, as Freud does, that bodily organs acquire a sexual meaning—*eine sexuelle Bedeutung*. It is this term, *Bedeutung*, that Lacan, preserving the original German, brought into relief with regard to the phallus, following Freud's expression *Die Bedeutung des Phallus* in his text in the *Écrits* which bears this title. Later on he tried to make an allusion to the logician, Frege, who also distinguished between *Sinn* and

Bedeutung. Nonetheless, I believe that the *Bedeutung* in Lacan's text is actually very directly Freudian, and that it can only be inserted in a Fregean set of concepts with great difficulty.

• THE ORIGINAL REFERENCE OF *JOUISSANCE*

From the point of view of *jouissance*, thc difference between perversion and hysteria is thus not essential. In perversion, substitution is live, it is fully displayed and is conscious: the subject knows what he is seeking, he knows what the action required is, the object he needs in order to enjoy. In hysteria, by contrast, this is unconscious. In order to find the sexual signification function, one must go through the detour of the interpretation of the symptom. But, aside from this difference regarding consciousness and unconsciousness, in both cases we are dealing with substitutive *jouissance*.

This conception of substitution by *jouissance*, of substitutive *jouissance*, is the basis of Freud's entire theory of the evolution of libido. When Freud highlights the erogenous areas and the corresponding objects—the oral object, the anal object—the erogenous areas with the organ pleasure which they entail and make possible, when he details the partial drives, it is always within the framework of the substitutive *jouissance*. The evolution of the libido shows that one must first pass through the substitutive *jouissance* before arriving at a *jouissance* which would no longer be substitutive.

What is this substitutive *jouissance*? There is, in Freud's work, a standard of substitution, an original reference of *jouissance*. Unfortunately, if I may say so, it's a later reference in what he calls the evolution of libido. The reference by which he measures substitutions is sexuality in its reproductive, procreative role—that of ordinary coition. Freud's reference is thus sexuality insofar as it follows the biological program. It is in relation to this that he only sees a substitutive *jouissance* in the history of libido. If you read Freud properly, you will see that *jouissance* is always substitutive, except when it follows the biological program. And he's not wrong at all in regarding coition as something that is always extraordinary!

Freud is led to suppose that there is a turn in the evolution of libido—that's how he puts it—in which all partial drives become subordinate to the primacy of the genital organs, they submit to the function of procreation. Partial drives stop gamboling, stop seizing suction, the gaze, the voice—the two objects added by Lacan—and focus on procreative sexuality. Otherwise put, for Freud—is there a simpler way of saying it—there is such a thing as a sexual relationship. The constant substitutions of *jouissance* are measured with respect to the existence of the sexual relationship.

• LACANIAN *JOUISSANCE* AND FEMININE LOGIC

After Lacan said that there is no sexual relationship, people have wondered about what he meant by sexual relationship. I have already explained it thirty-six times, but I believe I cannot explain it in a simpler way than by saying that Lacan calls sexual relationship what constitutes Freud's reference in his entire theory of libido, in his entire theory of the drives, and with respect to which he measure the substitutions of *jouissance*.

The consequence of the formula by which there is no sexual relationship is to sketch out an economics of *jouissance* which is substitutive through and through—with no original. That the sexual relationship does not exist means that there is no *ganze Sexualstrebung*, no total sexual drive, as Freud puts it. Lacan already denied it in Seminar XI. This is the translation of the fact that there is no sexual relationship. The *jouissance* of which the *parlêtre* is capable is always the unsuitable *jouissance*. We can always say of *jouissance*, in Latin: *Non decet*—it is not suitable. The only suitable *jouissance* would be that of the sexual relationship, which does not exist

• THE RULE OF THE NOT-ALL

Thus Lacan generalizes the substitutive economics of *jouissance,* which is the key to his entire theory of the drives. If you will follow me, I will say that he was only able to formulate things in

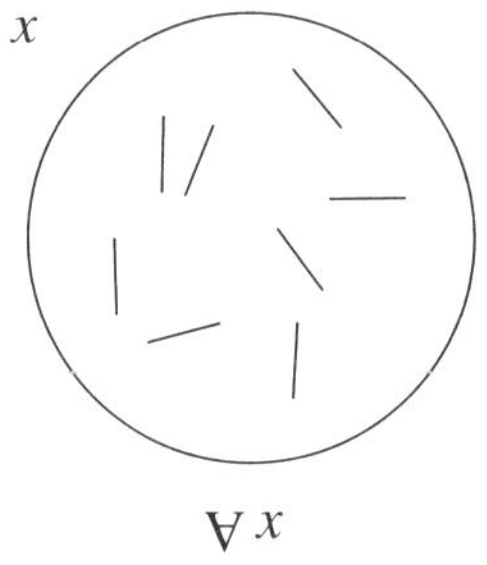

this way once he detached himself from the Freudian reference to structure feminine sexuality. Freud's theory of the drives follows the logic of masculine sexuation. It is a logic that is capable of totalizing the drives, of positing a for every x with regard to an element, a single referent, outside the class, which has a primacy and a privilege—the phallus—which is expressed in terms of power—Freud talks about the subordination of all the partial drives under the primacy of the genital organs.

The Freudian theory of the drives is Oedipal through and through, whereas the Lacanian theory of *jouissance* follows the rule of the not-all.

There is—I will write a zero between inverted commas here—no primacy of the phallus. There is not all for the drives—this is what I represent by means of a circle in dashes. There is rather a drive series, that of the substitutive *jouissance*—which I represent in my scheme with respect to the sexual relationship that

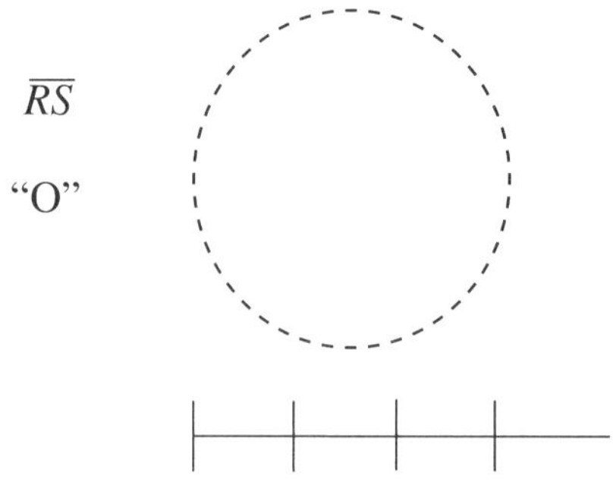

does not exist, by means of a series of segments. The Freudian element that gathers the entirety of the drives and subjects it is the sexual relationship. For Lacan, there is no sexual relationship—let us write it surmounted by a negation bar—thus there is only the series of substitutive *jouissance*.

Thus the theory of *jouissance* must be de-Oedipalized. It entails that what *jouissance* is given to us does not fit the sexual relationship. This is how *jouissance* constitutes a *sinthome*. Lacan's *sinthome* is simply the symptom, but generalized, the symptom inasmuch as there is no total sexual drive. It constitutes a symptom, but it's a symptom that is unavoidable.

On the basis of this fact, there is a metonymy running throughout this series of substitutive *jouissance*. The marvelous transformations of libido detailed by Freud find their place here; simply, they are not achieved, they are not closed in a unitary totality.

• *Jouissance* is everywhere

In this regard, if we remove its original reference, *jouissance* is everywhere in the signifier. There is a *jouissance* of speech, which is part of the metonymy of substitutive *jouissances*. There is a *jouissance* of knowledge, of the forbidden, etc. There is nothing within the sphere of the *parlêtre* to which a *jouissance* cannot be attached. Paraphrasing Leibniz, we might say: Nothing is without *jouissance*.

Hence the ridiculousness of the idea that psychoanalysis consists in abandoning *jouissance*, the idea of negativizing *jouissance*. All that we can say is that *jouissance* can be displaced, that it can be otherwise distributed. It can be metonymized in a different way, but it cannot be negativized—at least in the sense which I am proposing here.

There is a *jouissance* of the forbidden, there is a *jouissance* of knowledge, there is a *jouissance* of the body and there is also a *jouissance* of thought. Obsessional neurosis, for example, shows us the existence and the insistence of the *jouissance* proper to thought. *Jouissance* can be tracked down in all manifestations of interest. We might even say that nothing subsists for the *parlêtre* which does not have a *jouissance* coefficient. This is how the formation of symptoms is coextensive to the emergence of *jouissance*.

It is wrong of me however, at this point, to talk about emergence, as the *jouissance* in question is rather of the order of a surface, a surface crossed by waves, like the bells I spoke about. These waves measure for everyone the distance at which he or she stands from the sexual relationship which does not exist.

Love remains. Love, which Lacan does not tear from its imaginary root when he says that it is love that creates the illusion of a sexual relationship. This is what properly distinguishes *jouissance* and love. There is a *jouissance* in talking about love, in experiencing love, in writing love letters—or emails, obviously. This *jouissance* is at the same time the most distant and the closest one, topologically, to the sexual relationship which does not exist.

• On abjection

There is a word that Lacan was fond of. I know it better than anyone else. Once—this was 1966—when I had the galleys of the *Écrits* in front of me and was proofreading them, I told Lacan that an index of the concepts in his teaching should be made. He replied: Do it! I replied yes—it was easier to say yes to him than to say no. Nonetheless I had no idea of what that would involve. I had to make this index twice, as I also had the good idea of telling him to place the "Seminar on The Stolen Letter" at the start of the *Écrits*. I told him this because, if one followed the chronological order of the first set of galleys, the earliest texts were prior and external to his teaching proper. What I, or anybody else for that matter, had thought was that placing the "Seminar on The Stolen Letter" at the start of the *Écrits* would change the numeration of all the pages. The index which I had made for the first set of galleys was no longer any use when the second set arrived, with the "Seminar on The Stolen Letter" at the start.

Lacan's reply which I mentioned refers to the first set of galleys, when the decision to made an index of the concepts in the *Écrits* was made. He let me work as I wished, and just made one recommendation: "It must start with the word abjection." Unless I am mistaken, that is how the index starts. In any case, the word abjection is in there, this word which Lacan wished to be the alpha, if not the omega of his teaching.

• A CONTROVERSIAL SCOPE

This word, abjection, had a controversial scope. Indeed, Lacan found support in the idea that he was dealing with the abjection of his psychoanalyst colleagues. It was in this sense that this word is employed three times—if I recall rightly—in the *Écrits*. The word abjection also has a theoretical scope, inasmuch as the psychoanalyst, whether he or she is for or against Lacan, is assigned by Lacan to the position of the *objet a*. This object, as he said later, is also an abject.

Generally speaking, *jouissance* has its roots in abjection.

What are the opposites of this word? Dignity. Honor. Honor is only based on the signifier, which it brings to the ideal. This is what led Freud to extend his theory of the drives through the circuit of sublimation—the circuit taken by *jouissance*, which is ultimately abject, to attain the most touching realizations of the beautiful and the good.

When we say that *objet a* is only a piece of refuse, something that is rejected, we are actually saying that it is abject. It is an object of aversion, of disgust, of repulsion, but which at the same time produces surplus *jouissance*. In the analytic experience, what concerns what is most intimate about *jouissance* always takes the form of a confession—the confession of what deserves to attract, as the dictionary says, derision and opprobrium. Abjection is an extreme degree of lowering. The subject of the signifier, the subject of speech, does not even touch it, and only consents to confess his relation to it by bearing witness to the fact that repulsion accompanies, is inseparable from the invincible attraction that he experiences in this relation.

Being aware of Lacan's fondness for the word abjection once led me to read, and then to reread—maybe to revere—a little book which I think I have never spoken about here, by an author who is not one of my favorite writers for many reasons. This is someone who had the nerve to call his work *On Abjection,* a French author who, in the halcyon days of the NRF, was known for writing in an admirable French. Moreover, he was much admired in other countries, by German writers, for example—Ernst Jünger paid homage to him—which led him, it must be said, to admire Germany a little too much at a time when this power, now a friendly power, was occupying the French territory. There is no doubt that he knew something about abjection.

• Johandeau and Paulhan

This work is dedicated to another NRF luminary with whom Lacan also had some debates: Jean Paulhan, the author of *The Applied Warrior*. Marcel Jouhandeau thus dedicated his work to Paulhan, on the very verge of the disappearance of his book. This is the dedication: "My dear Jean, please accept this text as a document on anyone, which I have only agreed to give to you because I was tempted to destroy it."[2]

In the part which seems to concern anyone, that is, himself, Jouhandeau describes what he calls the monstrous tendency which he discovered in himself at the age of twelve, and which led him to decide to kill himself. He survived, only to hesitate between marrying and devoting himself exclusively to God—he was a very strong believer. He finally married, wrote horrible things about his wife, and gave himself over with a certain constancy, that is, with a certain frenzy, to his monstrous tendency, which nowadays seems pretty innocent—this book was written in 1939: homosexuality.

I recommend you read this work. Given that this is the last time that we meet in the course of this academic year, I will read you one of his passages, which is a variation on the topic "discovering one's own truth," which, these days, I understand as worthy of being included in the program of an analysis:

> Discovering one's own truth is not the same thing as guessing it or brushing past it or smelling its perfume or perceiving its reflection, admitting that it is ungraspable, or even understanding it to the point of being able to explain it: it means being possessed by it, despite oneself, not knowing why or how it is happening, from one's thumbnails and fingernails to the end of one's hairs, through all of one's senses to the depth of the soul, breathing nothing but it, seeing nothing but it, hearing and touching nothing but it in all things, obeying only it, addressing only it, desiring and fearing only it, being only one with it and it being one with you and the rest of the world of which it has become a sign only for you. And it matters little whether this truth is of a high order or a low order and whether it is "Truth" absolutely, as longs as it is uniquely yours or mine and that it inhabits me entirely. And it matters little whether I can explain it to myself, as long as it explains me to myself and the rest. Even if it has value only for me, if it is only accessible to me, as long as it gives the word enigma, as long as it determines each of my gestures, as long as it sets the pace of my steps, as long as it lights up my thoughts from within and galvanizes my words, animates my face, makes my tears flow, regulates my smile, commands the ineffable shadows of my sadness to cover me or to leave me: it is only this truth that delivers me to a pleasure that only I know, only this truth starts "my pleasure" in me; thanks to it I am no longer lost, in my search, in the search for my secret, I recover it; and even if I were the most unhappy of men and were I to pay for it with my damnation, I would prefer nobody in my impossibility to renounce truth: I mean, such memory, such emotion or such hope which I owe it, which confirm my stubbornness in remaining in the being and in my being, in wishing nothing at any cost other than my identity, my singularity.[3]

• Truth is *jouissance*

The truth that is dealt with by the short book from which this excerpt is taken—it's a book made up of fragments—which is also glimpsed in the declination of this truth, is *jouissance*. Let us note that, for the author, it was an infamous pleasure. We might take what is described there as the status of a subject after the crossing of the fantasm, except for the fact that Jouhandeau, it seems, never entered analysis and his truth should not be sought in the fantasm. What he writes takes place on the level of the *sinthome*, on the level of his entire life, to which he thinks *jouissance* gave its unity. What we call the *sinthome* can be taken for the unity of a life—not concentrated on the equivocal element that we call the fantasm.

To end the year, I wanted to read out this passage, which I believe is quite illuminating. If Lacan appealed to Paulhan's *Applied Warrior* to give us an idea of the pass as the crossing of the fantasm, I cannot see why I should not appeal to Jouhandeau to give us an idea of the pass on the level of the *sinthome*.

Jouhandeau also tells us how he managed his monstrous tendency. His arrangements culminated in the affirmation of his singularity, which might be called eternal, given that he enjoys his part in the gaze of the divine Being.

I will now leave Jouhandeau to try and take a perspective view of what I sought to explore this year, which appears when I look at what constitutes the thread, the support and torment of my intention: Lacan's teaching and the way in which I handle it today.

8. On the turns of saying and enjoying

Lacan's own support and thread was Freud's work. He qualified his project within psychoanalysis, the project of his teaching, as a Return to Freud. But this is not the last word. I will even go so far as to devalue the expression by seeing it as a slogan or the shibboleth of a propaganda in the circumstances in which Lacan had to take the ground. These circumstances were marked by the development in psychoanalysis of a conception which is nowadays rejected by all which called itself Ego Psychology. This was the way in which Freud's students, particularly emigrants to the United States, managed to translate Freudian concepts, privileging what is known as the second topology—which distinguishes ego, id, and superego—and reconfigured Freudian concepts around the idea of adaptation, turning, for example, the ego into a psychological function for adaptation to reality. This required keeping quite a distance from Freud's texts, which were replaced by the contributions of the Ego Psychology school, or by manuals of the orientation I mentioned.

• THE REVERSE OF FREUD'S PROJECT

Thus Lacan found himself in the position of making people read Freud at a time in which he could be regarded as surpassed. Thus the return to Freud could be understood as a return to the source. Lacan nonetheless said explicitly in the *Écrits* that a return to Freud in no way means a return to the sources, even if this was a byproduct of his action. He presented his first ten Seminars as commentaries on Freud, taking a text by Freud every year as his topic. His students at the time plunged into Freudian erudition, which produced the *Vocabulary of Psychoanalysis*. It was his students who were most involved in the return to the source that objected to Lacan's teaching after his first ten Seminars.

Lacan himself specified in what sense the "return to Freud" must be understood: taking the reverse of Freud's project.

He explained this reverse, this inversion, by means of the topological structure which he assigned to the subject—to simplify, the Moebius strip structure, which one can only walk through in its entirety on the condition of making a double turn which reverses one's orientation. Transposed to Freud's work, Lacan imagines that this double turn leads to a genuine elucidation. I quote him: "Everything must be resaid on the other side for what it encloses to be shut. One must not think that a totality is thus obtained or, as Lacan specifies, an absolute knowledge. He makes this double turn into the condition for, as he say, knowledge to reverse truth effects. I wonder whether this sentence has been properly printed, and whether it should not rather say reverse ("repay") instead, or renverse ("reverse"). Nonetheless, we can understand that a double turn is necessary for knowledge not to remain stuck in utterances which seem to be ne varietur and for truth to emerge from a reversal.

• A DOUBLE TURN

What is the substitution by which this double turn takes place? The only indication which I can decipher is that Freud remained imprisoned within a reference to the sphere, with regard to which inside and outside are distributed, whereas Lacan's turn replaced the sphere with topological surfaces which have a completely different distribution—topological surfaces such as the Moebius strip, Klein's bottle, and particularly the projective plan that is a transformation of the sphere.

I will not go into the details of the double turn that goes from Freud to Lacan, I am just inspired by the notion of taking the reverse to locate the dimension that is opened to us by what I called Lacan's last and very last teaching. These are not only chronological labels. There is—as I pointed out in recent years—a turning, a split, which finds an echo in what is transformed on an everyday basis in psychoanalytical practice.

I am inspired by what Lacan was able to extract from his relationship with Freud to propose that his last teaching, as well as his very last teaching that was its end, represent Lacan's taking the reverse of his own project. Lacan made it impossible for anyone to do to him what he did to Freud. In the same way as he said that he took the reverse of Freud's project by indexing it on the substitution of the sphere by topological surfaces, he himself substituted, in his last teaching, topological surfaces by Borromean knots. If we follow his indication to index his taking the project on the reverse of these spatial references, it is blindingly obvious that Lacan himself performed a substitution of the same sort.

What I am telling you is only the index of a reversal. What is this reversal? What can I say more clearly and concisely about it? The passage to the reverse in Lacan's teaching does not only concern this teaching, but also analytical practice as it is carried out—this is my hypothesis—in the space which he opened up, doubtlessly in order to be closer to what the transformations in practice where sketching out in his own times. Thus I am trying to be simple and will tell you what I came up with.

The first turn in Lacan's teaching puts forward and exploits the subordination of *jouissance* to the primacy of the structure of language. The passage to the reverse indicated by Lacan—which he did not accomplish with the same perfection as he did in his first turn—then consisted in the subordination of the structure of language to *jouissance*.

This is correlative to a displacement of what we agree to call analytic listening. But it goes much farther than listening! It involves the interpretation and aims of experience. The primacy of *jouissance* is not an abstraction. Concerning analytic practice, it involves placing the phenomena which appear in it—the analysand's speech and what it bears witness to—under the question: What does this satisfy? This question is quite different from the question: What does this mean? I see here a reversal, an inversion, a passage to the reverse which goes from signification to satisfaction.

Detaching oneself from the implications of the question "What does this mean?" opens up another dimension of saying which leads one, explicitly even, to seek where that enjoys. We say with Lacan—a Lacan who copies and transforms Descartes that the body is an enjoying substance. But this is not the final word. It is not only the body that enjoys. There is *jouissance* in speech, *jouissance* in thought, as all those who have described the phenomenon of obsessional neurosis have been led to note, in one way or the other. Language itself is a device for *jouissance*, and not only a device for the production of signification. The signifier is not only the cause of the signified, the cause of the subject, it also causes *jouissance*.

This leads to a status of the signifier prior to the structure of language, which can be called prelinguistic, if linguistics starts when signification effects are taken into account. It was along these lines that Lacan invented *lalangue*, woven with signifiers but prior to language. The structure of language appears as derived with respect to *lalangue*.

• The index of inertia

If there is such a passage to the reverse, we should also be able to find true indices of it. I have found one, which revolves around the term inertia.

I had already signaled the value and scope of this word, inertia, at the start of Lacan's teaching. I had highlighted the expression "the inertia of the imaginary factors," in the first page of the *Écrits* after the Introduction, the first page of the "Seminar on The Stolen Letter"—a stolen letter which bears witness to the structuring displacement of the signifier. Isolating the imaginary and assigning it a function of inertia in analytic experience is quite essential and structuring in the first turn of Lacan's teaching.

• The imaginary factors

For the first Lacan, the inertia attributed to the imaginary factors is opposed to the dynamics of the symbolic factors. He paid all his attention to highlighting the mechanisms which support these symbolic factors, reformulated on the basis of Freud's work: *Verwerfung* (foreclusion), *Verdrängung* (repression) and *Verneinung* (denial). These three terms appear in the first page of the "Seminar on The Stolen Letter," to which can be added *Verleugnung* (negation, if this translation can be accepted). By contrast to Ego Psychology, which focused on the imaginary factors, Lacan stood out for highlighting the symbolic dimension supported by the structure of language, as the location of a dynamics by which changes take place.

In what way are imaginary factors inertial? This is because, at Lacan's starting point, the imaginary was the locus of *jouissance*: the subject enjoys the imaginary. This imaginary is for Lacan primarily scopic; it is related to vision. For early Lacan, the body is not the enjoying substance, but above all the shape of the body. This inertia is precisely linked, in his teaching, to the discovery that he had made twenty years before—what he called the mirror stage, where there is the emergence of the little man's joy in front of his own reflection. The question was accounting for what leads him to *jouït* the image. For some time, Lacan organized what he captured about the analytic experience on the basis of this imaginary couple: the subject and his image.

When the first turn in his teaching started, Lacan relocated this imaginary relationship *a—a'* and located there the entire dimension explored by Ego Psychology: the ego is an imaginary effect, the narcissism and *jouissance* of this imaginary ego, and all that is fantasmatic was placed along the line of this relationship.

The mirror stage in a way subordinated what Lacan called the fantasmization revealed by the analytic experience. When his teaching started, all this represented what is inertial about experience. It is against this background that the dynamics of the symbolic coupe, which goes from the big Other to the subject, A-> S, appears, interposes itself, shields and puts a brake on the imaginary relationship. Lacan's entire early teaching consists in

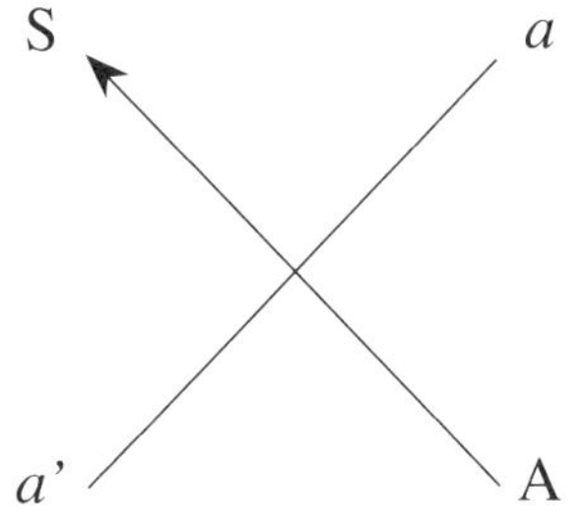

opposing the inertial imaginary couple and the symbolic intersubjectivity, which is dynamic.

• Rectifications

This is a prescription of what must be neglected in psychoanalytic experience in order to take an interest in signifiers as dynamic elements which weave a relationship between the subject and the Other, a relationship of positive symbolic identification which is distinct from imaginary identification. If we neglect what is symbolic about experience, and thus if we neglect interpretation, we only rectify the imaginary. Rectifying the imaginary is an expression used by Lacan, which evokes the concept of symbolic rectification in "The Direction of the Cure." Rectification is a delicate term, as it appeals to a rule, but Lacan, repudiating imaginary rectification, could only displace it onto the symbolic register. He even talked about orthodramatization: one must rectify—in the sense of ortho—the dramatization of one's experience by the subject. A practice that consists in rectifying the imaginary is a practice that is inspired in object relations. Lacan indicates in the *Écrits* that this practice, restricted to the imaginary, cannot but arouse a feeling of abjection in every man of good faith.

There is a decisive inspiration for the first turn in Lacan's teaching which I already find in his text "Intervention on transference," on the Dora case, in which transference is based on the imaginary couple. Transference is thought of as an imaginary formation, which emerges at a time of stagnation in psychoanalytic dialectics, which in turn developed along the symbolic axis.

The aim of Lacan's first Seminars was to systematically translate Freud's main concepts, presented by Ego Psychology as imaginary formations, in order to place them along the symbolic axis. Thus transference also became a symbolic effect, and so on. Lacan's early teaching took place as a symbolization of Freud's main concepts.

The word inertia must be taken as an index.

In the very first turn in Lacan's teaching, inertia is proper to *jouissance*, whereas the symbolic is dynamic. His last Seminar, *Encore*—when I undertook writing the series; will I finish it soon?—is the one which marks the moment of the passage to the reverse. We find in it the word inertia, which—and however simple this may be, it would have been impossible in the first turn—no longer qualifies the imaginary, but language itself. Said language involves considerable inertia, he says. This inertia in the functioning of language is thus opposed to the speed of mathematical signs, the mathemes which are easily transmitted, integrally, without knowing what they mean. We must understand that it is precisely because these mathematical signs– at least this is how I understand it—are free of signifieds, they do not have the inertia displayed by the functioning of language insofar as it is loaded with signifieds.

• Reversal

If we can see this, we will realize that the value of language changes through and through in this passage, and that Lacan was led into a sense in which the symbolic dynamics are exhausted and replaced by routine. This is illuminated in Seminar XX: If the signifier always has the same sense, it is due to routine. Sense is given by the feeling that everyone has of being a part of his world, his family, and everything revolving around it. We can see that the very notion of discourse, the discourses that Lacan created as the foundations of the social link, was already based on the idea of routine, on the idea that the signifying structure is actually as such intertial, that inertia is on the side of the structure of language. The association symbolic equals dynamic is thereby blurred. On the contrary, the symbolic appears as a routine, a discourse, a disc, a repetition. It is even because he linked language and inertia that Lacan was able to say that what seems to best support the idea of language is the idea of strings in circles. When he introduced the strings in circles which can be articulated among themselves, he introduced them as a representation of the inertia of language.

Thus take this inversion of inertia as an index.

By passing Freudian concepts into the symbolic, Lacan came, in Seminar VI, *Desire and Its Interpretation*, to such a reabsorption of the imaginary into the symbolic, that he then had, in another leap, to create another pole which he seized from Freud—he called it *das Ding* in his Seminar *The Ethics of Psychoanalysis*. It was already a sort of passage to the reverse, but he only dealt with this *das Ding* in his teaching—which, to avoid awkwardness, is a name for *jouissance*—as *objet a*, that is to say, by imposing the structure of language onto it. *Objet a* is precisely the mark of the subordination of *jouissance* to the structure of language—until this *objet a* is turned into a constant.

Lacan reduced the imaginary and inertial screen of his early teaching to the structure of the fantasm ($\$$ <> a). He put the fantasm in the same place, in an obviously much more elaborated fashion, as the model of the mirror stage. The best proof is that if we replace the imaginary vector with the fantasm in schema L—which I don't think I have done, although it is blindingly obvious!—we will understand the expression "crossing of the fantasm" so much better.

• THE DEVICE FOR *JOUISSANCE* IS LANGUAGE

What Lacan called the fantasm is the fundamental relationship with *jouissance* modeled by the structure of language—taking care to remark that if said fantasm has imaginary roots, the

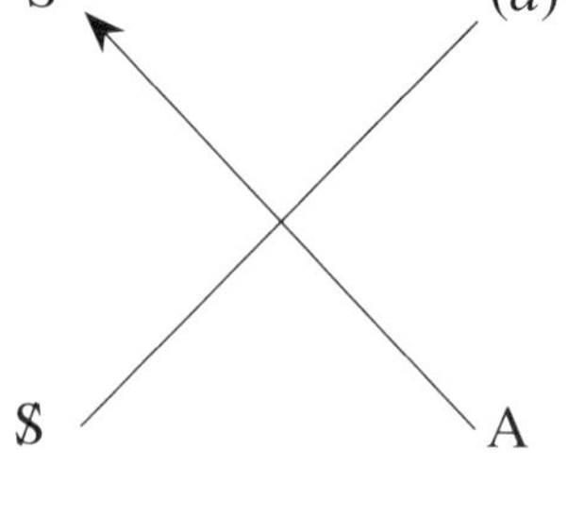

symbolic is nonetheless involved in the form of scenarios, inasmuch as it constitutes a window onto the real, inasmuch as it plays the role of the real.

The idea of the pass is based on the notion that the fantasm is the device for *jouissance*, that it is through this device that the subject approaches reality. In the passage to the reverse, the device for *jouissance* is no longer contained within the limits of the fantasm. It is language itself that appears as this device—one more step and it's *lalangue*, the signifier stripped from the structure of language. In the passage to the reverse, the *sinthome* takes the place of the fantasm. Which means that the fundamental relation to *jouissance* is no longer enclosed in the inertia and condensation of the fantasm, which must be crossed by a dynamics. It is in the *sinthome*, not as condensation but as functioning, that the symbolic, the imaginary, and the real are driven, involved, and bound.

Finally, if we look at Freud's lectures in *Introduction to Psychoanalysis*, we can see that he introduced his audience to psychoanalysis by highlighting, in the first two parts, the interpretation of Freudian slips and dreams, and then giving, in the third part, his theory of libido under the general title *A General Theory of Neurosis*. His landmark or reference was perversion. Perversion appears at the start of the *General Theory of Neurosis*, as displaying a condensation of *jouissance*: an abjection to which the subject cannot help but give himself—what is nowadays called an addition.

• The model of perversion

It is perversion that provides the model for *objet a*. Lacan also used perversion as a model to say that it's the same in neuroses as in perversion, although we do not realize it because it's camouflaged, scrambled by the labyrinths of desire, inasmuch as desire is a defense against *jouissance*. In neuroses, we must pass through interpretation.

Following the model of perversion, we do not pass through the fantasm. On the contrary, perversion highlights the place of a device, a functioning. This is what the concept of the *sinthome* shows. It is not condensed in a privileged location, which is called the fantasm. It takes, within its parentheses, life in its entirety. In the same way, *jouissance* is not only imprisoned within the small capture of *objet a*, but rather extends wherever there is a signifier. The major fact is achieving *jouissance*.

• *Jouissance*, sense and the pass

On this point, Lacan is different from Freud. Freud thinks of libido as energy, as something that can be described by an energetics. Lacan posits that *jouissance* does not constitute and cannot be described as energy. Energy can be calculated. It entails a mathematical structure. Yet if *jouissance* is consubstantial to the signifier, it is deciphered. Hence the notion which imposes itself—even if Lacan didn't formulate it like this—of the interpretation of *jouissance*.

The interpretation of *jouissance* is only a speculation of knowledge about *jouissance*, about the reason why it is not suitable. We know why it isn't suitable! It is not suitable because there is no such thing as Freud's norm, because the sexual norm, that of the sexual relationship, does not exist. What is interpreted are the contingent forms which this lack of sexual relationship has taken, particularly in the family and the parental couple.

Interpretation of *jouissance*, because if analytic discourse is aimed at sense, sense is nothing but the routine of a discourse, the routine of the environment in which you live. With respect to the sexual non-relationship, with respect to *jouissance*, this sense is a semblant.

What takes then the place of the crossing of the non-existent fantasm? The semblantization of sense, the reduction of this truth—which cannot be discovered—to lying truth. If the pass does not take place in relation to the fantasm but in relation to the *sinthome*, it is not the revelation of a truth. The pass is the revelation that truth lies, that sense is a semblance. What is elucidated is how *jouissance* is interpellated, by you, by the semblant, by the signified, or by the beautiful unforgettable form that Jouhandeau came across when he was twelve.

This pass of the *sinthome* also amounts to the eternal return of its singularity in *jouissance*. As in *The Applied Warrior,* we have here a *parlêtre* who is no longer tormented by the truth. Even this end is contingent. Maybe the end of analysis has the structure of a meeting.

Miller, J.-A., L'orientation lacanienne, "Choses de finesse en psychanalyse," 2008-2009: Teaching given at the Paris VIII university psychoanalysis department—course of the 13th and 20th May, 3 and 10 of June 2009. The text has been transcribed and established by Jacques Péraldi, edited by Nathalie Groges-Labedbrichs and Yves Vanderveken for *La Cause freudienne*. Not reread by the author.

1. Poe, E.A, "Lange du bizarre", Histoires grotesques et sérieuses, translated by Charles Baudelaire, Paris, Classiques, 1973
2. Jouhandeau, M., De l'abjection, Paris, Gallimard, 2006.
3. Ibid. p. 26-27.

Chapter 8
Women and Families
(445e—471c)

ALAIN BADIOU

translated by SUSAN SPITZER

A BRIEF INTRODUCTION

At a certain point in the dialogue, when discussing the "guardians," Socrates had advocated a strictly egalitarian life, along with the abolition of private property. One of the young people had then asked: "But what should be done about women and children?" And Socrates replied: "Friends share everything in common." Then he went on to another subject.

Much later, Socrates' listeners still remember that somewhat mysterious answer. And just as he's about to discuss the bad systems of government, they force Socrates to explain what he meant. This is essentially what's at stake in Chapter 8.

It was getting darker and darker. Here and there, the oil lamps were describing little circles within which the light was bravely flickering. Socrates was about to go over the four deficient systems of government in the logical and historical order that governs their interrelationship when Polemarchus touched Amantha's bare shoulder. The stern young woman bridled at first, then understood that he only wanted to get her attention. She leaned in closer to him, and he whispered in her ear:

—Are we going to let him get around the obstacle as though he hadn't even seen it?

—No, we definitely have to keep him from doing so, Amantha replied.

—Keep who from doing what? said Socrates, turning around.

—You—said Amantha—from treating us like fools.

—Oh, damn! What've I done?

—You treat us with an inexcusable lack of seriousness, if you don't mind my saying so, replied a very irate Amantha. You skip over a question of the utmost importance just so you don't have to get your feet wet. Do you think you can get off the hook by casually dropping into the conversation that, where women and children are concerned, it's clear that—let me quote that phrase of yours—"friends share everything in common"?

—But, my dear Amantha, isn't that true?

—Unless it's some kind of obscenity, I, as a young woman, have no idea what that sentence even means: what exactly is supposed to be "shared in common"? We've been badgering you for ages now to expound your views on sexual difference, procreation, and the upbringing of young children. But every single time you've been indirect and evasive.

—She's right, Polemarchus chimed in. Once, you practically laughed in our faces, and I quote: "I'm like old Tolstoy. When he was asked what he thought about all this, he replied that he wouldn't say the last word on women until the lid on his coffin was closed!"

—You're not going to move on to the study of the four non-communist systems of government without first explaining inside out and upside down everything related to sex, Amantha continued with increasing vehemence.

—I have to say, added Glaucon, that I won't let you sneakily bypass this crucial issue either.

And suddenly even Thrasymachus revived, probably because he'd heard the word "sex," and spoken by a woman at that:

—You're really in big trouble now, Socrates, he crowed. Whenever we finally get around to concrete questions, Socrates, as I've always said, ducks them.

Pressed from all sides like this, our hero put on a pleading face and said:

—What are you up to, my friends? What kind of quibbling are you starting up again, at the darkest edges of collective life? I did actually think I'd cleverly avoided these questions about sex and that you'd therefore settle for my brief references to equality. But now you're stirring up a hornet's nest—it'll take us the next two days to deal with all this!

—So what if it does? said Thrasymachus, who was now completely awake and completely sarcastic. Do you think we're spending the night in this big villa just to snore away contentedly or listen to platitudes? If sex is on the agenda now, you have to explain your sexual theory to us, period.

—But with this type of subject, said Socrates in self-defense, the discussion always goes on for an inordinate length of time.

—When it comes to sex, dear friend, replied Thrasymachus, who was dead set on sticking it to him, there are no time limits. An entire lifetime wouldn't be enough to cover the topic adequately, so fascinated is everyone by it. So never mind about us. Just answer our questions for once, expound your doctrine on the education of women, including sex. Don't act like the uptight philosopher, don't shy away from the stuff about nudity and fucking. And also tell us how the awful drudgery of babies and toddlers should be handled. You'll see what our reaction is.

—He's right, Socrates, Glaucon agreed. Your listeners tonight are educated, open-minded people, prepared to accept the most revolutionary new ideas. Put your suspicions and fears aside.

—You think you're reassuring me by saying that, but you're only increasing my anxiety. If I had complete confidence in myself about the real knowledge underlying what I say, your encouraging words would be very welcome. When you're speaking before a sympathetic, well-versed audience, either you really know a few truths about important matters that are close to your most cherished concerns and then you can speak calmly and confidently, or else you speak without having the least bit of certainty and you formulate more questions than answers, which is my way of doing things, and then you find yourself in a situation that's not exactly ridiculous—it would be childish to feel that way—but risky and precarious, because not only might you be straying far, very far afield from the truth but you might also be dragging your friends along with you to boot, on issues where that kind of straying comes with a very high price. On account of what you're trying to force me to say, I kneel trembling before the big Other, the distinguished judge of sexual matters. We're well aware that, in the Other's eyes, involuntary manslaughter is a lesser crime than misleading people about what's noble, good, and just in collective life. But if that crime has nevertheless got to be committed, as you would have me do, it would be better to be dealing with enemies than friends. That's why pushing me to my limits isn't a good thing, no, it's really not.

Glaucon greeted this speech with a loud guffaw:

—My dear Socrates, even if your speech were to exile us from the country of truth we'd acquit you of murder, and, by the same verdict, of fraud. So you can speak without fear of having to drink the fatal hemlock.

Socrates then awed his audience with a lengthy silence, his face a frozen, inscrutable mask. At last he relaxed and said with a broad smile:

—It's true that, according to our laws, anyone acquitted of murder regains his innocence completely. So the same will hold for me if you acquit me of fraud, right?

—Of course, Glaucon agreed. You have no further reason for remaining silent.

—Unfortunately! I, the philosophical stage director of male roles, shall now have to deal with the female roles so that the play can be performed...

—And that's a lot different, isn't it? said Amantha ironically.

—Not as much as all that, young lady, not as much as all that! After all, our conception of the development of everyone's leadership abilities has nothing whatsoever to do with sex. On the contrary, it assumes that we attribute to women a basic nature and ways of being that are more or less the same as men's, even if it means we then have to examine whether this principle can really work.

—Yeah, it has to be examined closely, whined Glaucon.

—Honestly, you're such an idiot! a furious Amantha protested. Think back to the comparison that was made between the temporary leaders of our communist country and clever, faithful guard-dogs guarding a peaceful flock of ordinary citizens—from which the "guardians" come, of which they're merely a detachment. Your idea wouldn't happen to be that the female dogs are only good for bearing puppies and that the protection and leadership duties have to be reserved for the males, would it?

—That's not what I said, but…

—Well, buddy, if you think women can do the job the same as men can, don't you have to feed them, train them, and educate them exactly the same as men?

—Socrates, Glaucon pleaded, is that really what you think?

—I have no choice… If we expect women to provide the same services, in terms of the community's future, as men, we have to give them the same basic education. We based the education of our "guardians," meaning all our citizens, on literature, music, and physical training, and there's no reason to change that curriculum just because we're dealing with women. The same will moreover hold true later on when we talk about higher education, and about mathematics and dialectic in particular. It'll be to everyone's benefit!

—And women'll do military training too?

—Definitely. We hope to put an end, for good, to the monstrosity of those wholesale slaughters called "wars." But if we're attacked, we'll defend ourselves.

—With women at the forefront, said Amantha approvingly.

—That's what I've always said.

—But really! Glaucon persisted. What about modesty, the difference between the sexes, sexual desire? It's common practice for men to train in the nude, shower together in the locker room and tell really dirty jokes, all that kind of stuff... Can you see beautiful, naked young women in the midst of a bunch of bozos like that? Honestly, can you see that?

Socrates adopted a half-stern, half-dreamy tone:

—Dear Glaucon, in our country there won't be—no, there'll never be—just a handful of naked women in the midst of a whole flock of men. But there'll definitely be the love between a woman and a man, in the refuge of their private lives. Besides which there'll be humanity as a whole, women, old people, young men, black, heavy, white, light, cross-eyed and hunchbacked, yellow, wan, glowing with health, every conceivable kind of body, as mixed as they are different from one another, bodies whose possible nudity will mean nothing other than jointly performing the same drills requiring nudity (a very rare requirement, as I see it). Every individual will get over the particular differences involved in one or another of these joint drills whatever way he can, but with the same degree of enthusiasm.

Amantha suddenly remembered the literature she'd read in secret:

—If our dear old Aristophanes were to see one of those "very rare" nude co-ed drills he'd find plenty of material in it to beef up the furious speech of his male chorus leader. Do you remember in *Lysistrata*?

If manly you men don't stand up tall
But give in to the race of the shrew,
With just their bare hands they will all
Spread the seeds of the blackest coup.

They will sharpen their knives with a will.
Nor to cut off our balls will they quail.
Our briefs to the brim will they fill
With shit they'll bring home by the pail.

Riding his prick, astride him, her steed:
This a man must have seen in his life
To fathom what darkness can breed
In the heart of his wanton wife.

—Well, said Socrates playfully, I see you have quite an extensive repertoire. But Aristophanes is not going to distract us from saying that women can and must—naked, if required by the oddity of the situation—pilot our fighter planes, command our assault tank divisions, and be in charge stealthily, beneath the waves, of our nuclear submarines. The truth is, hiding or exhibiting this or that part of the body is only a matter of the contingency of customs. It's stupid to hit the ceiling just because a woman shows her thighs, but it's no less so to make laws, as the French do, prohibiting a woman from covering her hair with a headscarf. Only brainless idiots find something that's merely a custom different from their own to be ridiculous or scandalous. We ought to be suspicious of anyone who wants us to be outraged about trivial things like this and not about what's truly insane or dangerous, namely, having intentions that are completely opposed to the Good that can be derived from the available truths.

—That kind of blowhard is usually an unwitting fascist, said Amantha sharply.

—But our main concern is to agree on the issue of whether our ideas are feasible or not, and, to that end, to summon an interlocutor who will discuss them—as happily as a lark or as soberly as a judge—and attempt to find out whether the female branch of the human species is capable of sharing all the tasks of the male branch, or none of them, or only some of them, and to what category of tasks everything having to do with war should be assigned.

—With a method as innovative and clever as that, snickered Amantha, we're bound to come to a brilliant conclusion.

—Go ahead and laugh! Socrates retorted. Or rather, why don't you play the part of the stubborn interlocutor, the guy who's sure that, thanks to him, we're going to fall flat on our faces.

—Gladly.

So Amantha took on the shrill voice of a law professor:

—Dear Socrates, dear Glaucon, there's no need for other people to challenge your conclusions: you disagree with each other enough as it is. When you summarized the true nature of a country and its government, you emphasized the division of labor and acknowledged that the taste for a given occupation had to do with each person's natural talents.

—Of course we did, objected Socrates, but often, when spurred on by you, we revised our analysis in a communist direction: everyone has to be able to handle everything.

—But certainly not to the point of disregarding a natural,

symbolic difference as crucial as sexual difference, Amantha continued in a very pedantic tone. Will you deny the ontological nature, so to speak, of that difference, gentlemen?

—Not at all, Glaucon piped up. Women and guys have virtually nothing in common.

—So, gentlemen, the noose of contradiction tightens around your argument and strangles all the life out of it. It's absurd to argue, on the one hand, that the State must be ruled in a way that's as appropriate as possible to its unique nature, and that, to that end, a workforce as homogeneous as it is skilled, coming from the masses of ordinary workers, must be trained, and, on the other hand, that both the subjective and objective difference between men and women can simply be ignored as far as all this is concerned. Can you clear up that inconsistency for us all, dear brother?

—Well, off the top of my head, I don't have an answer.

—What about you, Socrates?

—I've been saying all along that the question of the sexes is a labyrinth worse than the Minotaur's.

—And what's more, that guy Theseus needed a woman to get out of it.

—Ah yes, Ariadne, the eternal abandoned woman... Can you see why I'm tempted to abandon this discussion?

—But you won't, said Amantha.

—Oh, you know me so well. After all, whether you fall into a duck pond or the Pacific Ocean, all you can do is swim. So let's take the plunge and hope that, as with the poet Arion in the legend, a dolphin will take us on his back and set us down safe and sound on the rock on Cape Taenarum.

—What an adventure! joked Amantha.

—Dealing with one woman alone is already a wild and

woolly adventure for a man. So all women at once...

—You can do it, Socrates! Confront those monsters!

—Well, if you're ordering me to... Let's see now, let's recap the problem. If human beings have truly different natures, it's unlikely that they'll be suited for the same tasks in the same way. Now, men and women do have different natures. Therefore, we can't conclude, as we did, that if they're educated in the same way men and women will accomplish the same leadership tasks equally effectively. Is that right?

—Absolutely, replied Glaucon, and I really don't see how we're going to find a way out of this.

—False dialectic, the dialectic that's nothing more than the skillful manipulation of contradictions, is sure as hell powerful.

—Huh? What are you talking about? asked a surprised Glaucon.

—A lot of people unwittingly rush into this kind of dispute and imagine they're really dialecticizing when all they're doing is squabbling with each other. Why? Because they're incapable of resolving a problem on the basis of the immanent multiplicity of ideas it contains. For them, the process of countering an opponent remains at a purely verbal level, and so the whole discussion is merely a matter of contentious sophistry, not dialectic.

—Fine, fine, grumbled Amantha, but what does that have to do with the business about sex?

—We, too, may very likely be the unwitting victims of pseudo-counter-arguments. Grounding ourselves in the supposed self-evidence of the words "man" and "woman," we object to one other, with a suspicious sort of enthusiasm, that the same tasks can't suit natures that are so different from each other, but we haven't examined beforehand the idea we have about both that difference and that sameness, nor what type of relationship we have in mind when we attribute different tasks to different natures and similar tasks to similar natures.

—Can you give some examples other than men and women? asked Glaucon, really bewildered.

—To begin with, ask yourself whether, among the males of the human species, the bald ones and the ones with hair have the same nature or whether they constitute two mutually exclusive groups. Then, once you've observed that there's a real difference between them, draw the conclusion that the bald men must not be allowed to fish if we see that many men with hair are good at it.

—You've got to be kidding!

—Not at all. I want to stress this. When we determine that there's a difference between people, we've got to beware right away that it's practically never a question of an absolute difference. The kind of difference we're talking about is relevant to the tasks that we claim it's important for. "Bald" or "with hair" surely constitutes a significant difference as regards the quality of being "a hair stylist's client" but an insignificant one when it comes to fishing. When we say that someone has a natural talent for medicine and that someone else has a talent for archery, that doesn't mean they're different in all respects. It may very well be that they're equally good at mathematics. When we claim that, in humanity considered as a whole, the sub-group of women differs from that of men, we need to specify with respect to which skill, to which task we're conceiving that difference, in order to ultimately attribute the monopoly of the said task to one sex or the other. If it appears that the sexes only differ in regard to the material process of reproduction—the females bear and give birth to children, while the males just deposit their seed in the woman's womb—there's nothing about that that can convince us that men and women differ as to political skill, and so we'll stick with our point of view: the "guardians" in charge of the country's affairs at any given moment can just as easily be female as male guardians.

—I'm not sure that that will suffice to shut up all the big macho males who think women are only good for sewing, cooking, cleaning, wiping kids' asses, vacuuming, and spreading their legs, protested Amantha.

—Well, let's once again ask our opponent, the disciple of Aristophanes and the whole reactionary clique, to tell us what the skill or task, in the political realm, is that's only suitable for men, and which women have no natural talent for. I'm waiting...

—He'll skirt the issue, groused Amantha. He'll whine, like Glaucon did just now, that it's a tricky question and off the top of his head he can't come up with an answer.

—So then, said an accommodating Socrates, let's ask him to follow along with us in the twists and turns of the demonstration whereby we're going to prove that, as far as governing a country is concerned, there's no task that should be reserved for one sex in particular.

—Go on! I'll play the reactionary, said Amantha gleefully.

—When you say that someone is good in a given field and that someone else isn't, don't you mean that the former catches on easily to what it's about while the latter is at a total loss?

—Well, what else could I possibly say? brayed Amantha.

—And also that the one who's good at it, after studying it for only a short time, is able to come up with things well beyond anything he's been taught, while the one who's lousy at it, after studying it for ages, can't even remember what he's been taught?

—He's wacko, this Socrates dude. If the only thing a guy can say is that if someone who's lousy is lousy, then the brainiac's smart—well, honestly, that's just too much.

—We can also say that in the one, the body is at the service of the intellect, while in the other, it's an obstacle to it, can't we?

—Now you're really mucking up the waters! What's this "intellect" of yours? What do you do with your intellect? In the sack, you've got to get it up, not intellectualize.

—But that's just it, my dear pimp: where does sex come into anything we've been talking about?

—We said it ages ago: thinking's fine, but getting a hard-on's better. Hence, sex is everywhere.

—Which is tantamount to saying it's nowhere. With the criteria we're using, it's very clear that in lots of different fields many women are better than a lot of men, but it's also clear that many men are superior to lots of women. And so nothing can be concluded except that, when it comes to governing a country, there's no task that's appropriate for women qua women, or appropriate for men qua men. Natural talents have been distributed equally between the two sexes, and consequently women are naturally fit for all tasks, just as men are.

—And yet there are loads of chicks who are lousy at math and very few, maybe even none at all, who are, I don't know, chiefs of staff, Amantha ventured pretty lamely, in her role as the obligatory misogynist.

—But differences like that are obviously the result of prejudices that have affected the education of girls for centuries, to the detriment of equality between the sexes. As for us, we'll maintain that every task should be open to women as well as to men. We'll say quite simply that some women are good at medicine and others are less so, some women love music and others don't much care for it, some women are extremely attracted to the art of war and others are disgusted by it, some women are philosophers and others prefer sophistry, some women are brave and other women are fearful… exactly like men. Our obligatory conclusion will be that nothing should prevent any woman from filling a position of leadership when it's her turn to do so. Both women and men can possess a nature suited to the defense of the country, and if that nature has seemed weaker in women for such a long time it's because it was deliberately atrophied in them by ruthless educational segregation and insidious propaganda about the so-called "weakness" of the female sex.

—Whereas everyone sees that we're more resilient than men, Amantha, who had turned back into herself, triumphantly crowed.

—That's very true. And there's nothing better in politics than the commitment of all those women who are as resilient as they are remarkable. This excellence in women will be enhanced, from childhood on, by literature, poetry, music, and physical training, as we've outlined their use in our academic curriculum.

—Which implies that, if necessary, we'll have to strip naked, like the males, said Amantha coyly.

—Of course. But a woman who's forced to strip naked

because one task or other in the service of the community requires it will have all the clothes she needs in her militant virtue. As for the men who might then be tempted to make off-color jokes, we'll say, like Pindar, that "they are picking the unripe fruit of laughter." Those males stupidly laugh about the very same thing that they themselves are doing, on the ridiculous pretext that a woman is doing it too. They'd be better off sticking with the saying "What benefits us is as beautiful as what harms us is ugly."

—And with inwardly rejoicing, said Amantha in conclusion, that the benefit of a drill can be symbolized by female nudity, which has always been the very image of beauty.

On that point Socrates could only agree with the young woman.

—So that concludes this chapter, as I see it. The wave that arose from this old business about the role of women and their education hasn't overwhelmed us in the least. Absolute equality between men and women from this perspective is not only a question of principle for us but we're also able to prove that it's the most beneficial thing for the community as a whole.

But Glaucon, for his part, didn't think that the communist lawmaker was out of the woods quite yet:

—There's still another wave that could drown us for good this time.

—What wave is that?

—What becomes of that primordial unit of society, the family, in your conception of things? Who'll take care of the children? And incidentally, in this context, what becomes of equality between women—who carry the unborn child in their wombs, who nourish the fetus with their own blood, who give birth in pain, who nurse the baby—and men, who had nothing to do with the whole business other than just screwing and coming? But above all, in your conception of things, what becomes of the family? The family, as we know, is the place where all the wealth is concentrated and where, in an absolutely unjustified way, it's passed on to individual heirs and not to the community as a whole, even if it's a matter of factories, banks, artistic treasures, apartment buildings, forests...The family seems to me to be absolutely necessary for raising children, while at the same time—since it's complicit with the worst aspects of private property—it's a pillar of an inegalitarian society and, what's more, the fetish of every reactionary system of government without exception. What do you have to say about such a paradox, Socrates?

—And let's not forget, added Amantha, Engels' wonderful book *The Origin of the Family, Private Property and the State*. That "origin" is common to all three terms and is responsible for the most decisive victory of oppression in the whole history of humanity. We've decided to abolish the private appropriation of everything that's useful and valuable for the community as whole. We've decided to dissolve the State by having everyone in turn fill all public positions. So what could make us hesitate in the face of that reactionary idol, the family? It needs to be completely abolished. It's the family that gives substance to the truly obscene ideas of patrimony, inheritance, heredity, superiority on the basis of birth, blood or race, necessary inequalities... Gide was right to exclaim: "Families, I hate you!"... Well, Socrates, cat got your tongue?

Socrates in fact just sat there, as though he were far

away. He mopped his brow. The silence persisted and the young people, feeling uneasy, didn't dare break it. Finally, Socrates said softly, almost under his breath:

—Your elder brother Plato thought he could speak in my name about this strange, almost intractable subject, the family. He took off, it's true, from a few careless remarks of mine, and he has me say roughly the following—I'm quoting from memory—: "Women will be shared in common by all the men. None of them will live privately with any one man. Children will also be shared in common. Fathers won't know who their children are, nor will children know who their fathers are." Yes, but in that case, what's responsible for amorous encounters, sexual relationships, the symbolic order of inheritance? The answer Plato attributes to me is: the State, always the State, forever the State. You were right to quote Engels, dear girl. But what's happened since then? In the Soviet Union, they abolished private property, but they made the State, which was supposed to wither away, stronger, and the family remained strong enough that the children of Party officials became the beneficiaries of hereditary privilege. And according to your brother's Socrates, in the ever-so-famous "ideal City," private property and the family are abolished, but the State emerges from these abolitions with exorbitant powers. On the basis of the axiom whereby children belong to the entire community, you end up, in line with this Platonic anti-family policy, with what can only be called horrors. Marriages are decided upon by the State, which institutes a rigged lottery so that the most beautiful human animals will become couples, the way it's done with pedigree dogs or plow oxen. And it's all so as to make sure you get "beautiful children." What's more, any newborns in whom a handicap, even a negligible one, is detected are discreetly murdered by the police. Brother-sister incest is legal, even recommended, since it's expected that the offspring of the inbreeding between two beautiful, intelligent adults will be beautiful and intelligent as well. The number of children you can have is set by the State. If you don't reach the limit, what happens is like what used to happen with the objectives set for the five-year plans in the Soviet Union: they investigate, they find the culprits, and they punish them. And if you go above the limit, you're not raised to the rank of national hero, like the coal miner Stakhanov in Stalin's day: you're punished too.

—But children aren't the same as coal, after all, said Amantha. Does a guy who fucks like a champion or a woman who's pregnant every ten months absolutely have to be decorated?

—That's not funny, Socrates protested angrily, though still in a soft voice, his face expressionless. Bear in mind that, in this ideal City, old people have the virtually limitless right to beat up on the young. Just think, to train children to serve the State, Plato claims you have to take them from the time they're five years old right into battle, so they can get used to being stoic when people's throats are slit, or they're disemboweled, or decapitated, and when they wade in blood and stumble over dismembered corpses. No, none of that is very funny.

—The brilliant French psychoanalyst Jacques Lacan, said Glaucon (very proud of himself for having this reference), who was nevertheless a great admirer of both Plato and you, said that the ideal City resembled "a well-kept horse breeding stable." So do you basically agree with him?

—I can understand how your brother, annoyed by the sort of resistance the family puts up to any revolutionary zeal, went to extremes and couldn't see any solution other than virtually total state control of personal relationships and the abolition of private life. Militant fraternity in the Party being more important than family solidarities, yes, I get how you can want such a thing. But what I can't go along with are the consequences of that vision, which are well-known by now. Children denouncing their fathers as "counter-revolutionaries," knowing that they'll be executed, and doing so not on account of fear but in the fervor of political duty: I can see a kind of terrible esthetics of the new world in that, a convulsive vision of "the new man." But the fact remains that there's something horrific about it, and it has no chance of enduring.

—But we saw that sort of thing again in the 60s of the 20th Century, Amantha reminded him. Some revolutionary groups advocated a totally collective lifestyle, in communal apartments, with open, public, non-exclusive sex. Desire was legitimate in and of itself, and there was nothing more moral than giving in to it. Everyone was like brothers and sisters, they screwed indiscriminately, without any regard for who their current partner was. That was the way it was, at least in the beginning, with the American Weathermen, some brave young people who wanted to rally Chicago's white proletarians to the cause of the revolution, and who, in despair over the failure of their efforts, resorted to setting off bombs here and there, ultimately ending up in prison for the rest of their lives.

Sometimes I look on those times with envy.

—Well, you're wrong to, said Socrates. No, that's all disastrous, it all leads nowhere. Dear friends, I, Socrates, won't pay that price for the necessary dissolution of the family such as it is. No, absolutely not. Taking advantage of the opportunity given me here by Badiou, I solemnly protest your brother Plato's interpretation of my thinking.

—But what then? Glaucon asked anxiously. Are we at a dead-end?

—We can always begin by drastically limiting inheritances. That would already be pretty good. In only a few generations, everything that deserves to would return to the sphere of collective ownership. As for the rest, let's face it, this question of the family and the dialectics of private and public life is the cross that communism's got to bear, because love, which is truth, too, requires withdrawal, requires that a certain share of invisibility be granted it. We can't pursue the path that would involve eliminating all distinction between public and private life simply because of the very real reactionary burden that family life represents. Moreover, the threat doesn't just come from communist ventures. Corrupt democracy—the political regime of decrepit capitalism—also loves "transparency," and the politicians expose their trifling love affairs, or even their orgies, to public view. The desire to eradicate love's creative secrets was blatant in the countries where it was declared that politics was "in command," that it had to sweep everything away before it. But it's just as much at work in countries where money's in command: the secret gratuitousness of love infuriates the capitalists who govern in that case; they much prefer the lucrative public profits of pornography. In both cases, they object to the fact that, where all non-political truths are concerned, withdrawal, silence, a refuge apart are necessary. This is true, after all, for artists and mathematicians, too. Yet this issue of withdrawal, of the separation between private and public life, has had family life as its dominant form from the origins of humanity. Even the greatest lovers can't avoid the need to create that kind of refuge for their private lives. And the result of this love-with-a-refuge is that, when children are born, they're welcomed into the grace of privacy, not mercilessly exposed to the tumult of public indifference. That's why, in the final analysis, the elimination of the family is both necessary and extremely difficult. Let's bear this cross, young people, and move on. We'll have to bear it until such time as the real evolution of things has given rise to the idea we're currently lacking where this issue is concerned.

—In short, said Amantha ironically, when it comes to the family, love's intimate power leads you to Wittgenstein's maxim: "Whereof we cannot speak we must remain silent."

—Let's say, instead, that we're waiting for the day when, with regard to the family and its truly complicated relationship to love and children, we'll finally be able to think: whereof we cannot speak we must do.

Lacan and Feminine *Jouissance*

Éric Laurent

translated by Marcus Andersson

We will begin by considering Lacan's formulation in "L'Étourdit" of the feminine position as a superego position. This position starts from the *jouissance* of the subject and develops a call from this presence of *jouissance*.

To elucidate this claim, Lacan plays the part of the Greek sphinx, ventriloquizing its voice:

> "You have satisfied me, littleman. You have understood, of *étourdit* there is not too much, for it to return to you in the *après midit*. Thanks to the hand that will respond to you, insofar as Antigone you call it, the same that can tear you apart because I *sphynge* my *notall*, you will be able even toward evening to make yourself the equal of Tiresias, and like him, from having made the Other, to divine what I have said to you."
> It is the superegohalf (*surmoitié*) that does not superego as easily as the universal conscience.
> Its *dits* would not know how to complete themselves, refute themselves, make themselves inconsistent, undemonstrate themselves, undecide themselves except in departing from what ex-sists of the paths of its *dire*.[1]

The sphinx begins by putting her *jouissance* first. She says: "You have satisfied me." She does not begin by saying: "I, the voice of truth, am speaking..." She, in other words, does not start from an enigma, where truth is immediately privileged. She begins directly by saying: "You have satisfied me, littleman." And she adds: "You have understood, that is what was required." But what did the littleman understand? We ask ourselves this because, at the end of the monologue, she tells him: "You will be able even toward evening [...] to divine what I have said to you."

"Go, of *étourdit* there is not too much, for it to return to you in the *après-midit*." The *après-midit* is a pun: it condenses the midday (*le midi*) of Oedipus and Lacan's half-said (*mi-dire*): "Truth can only speak half of itself, reveal itself in a half-saying."[2] If it is a question of the *après-midit*, it is because what precedes it is a *midit*. What follows the *midit* is what follows the Sphinx's first words: "You have satisfied me, my dear—finally, littleman; you have understood me, this is good."

So what is the *étourdit*? It is the mobilization of the chains of language, of the Other. It is the circuit of the said (*les tours du dit*). Lacan often uses the metaphor of the "circuit" to signify the geometrical torus, in which long winding coils wrap around the void encircled by language. This void is what language is incapable of expressing and what the holes of demand represent. Because language identifies the hole of desire.

"[...] for it to return to you [...]."

What could return to him? It could be something related to her *jouissance*, given that we do not know what returns to him. She is satisfied, but the only thing he has is his comprehension. While he's at it, he might like to have his part of the feast. This is why "[...] of *étourdit* there is not too much, for it to return to you in the *après-midit*," i.e. after the fact (*après-coup*): that precisely what you understood will return to you.

"Thanks to the hand that will respond to you… " Provided, the littleman calls and, in response, a hand comes to retrieve him. But this hand of Anitgone's is the one that accompanies Oedipus, with slashed eyes, beginning again in the night of his life, supporting himself with a cane and giving his hand to Antigone, having attained his *jouissance* and having seen what he had done.

"[…] insofar as Antigone you call it, the same that can tear you apart because I *sphynge* my *notall,* (*pastoute*)." It is strange indeed that Antigone's hand summons the littleman only to offer support, when it could just as easily destroy him.

"[…] because I *sphynge* […]" The verb, *sphynger*, was not adopted by the French language. One can understand it as "I pretend." Because there is something dissimulating about the "Sphynx." This part of the sentence can thus be understood as follows: "[…] because I mask myself, in the mask of the Sphynx, the quantifier of the not-all." In other words, in the end, the enigma that faces Oedipus is: Is there a *jouissance* beyond Oedipus, beyond phallic value? Because the feminine Sphynx asks those who pass to identify as men. The enigma addressed to Oedipus is: "You, who do not know who you are, make haste to identify as a man before I tear you to shreds." And Oedipus responds to this by identifying with the Phallus. But, later on, in Colone, far away from Thebes, Oedipus speaks of the beyond of simply having been the one who satisfied Jocasta. In this way, Antigone's hand could very well be, inexplicably, the hand of the sphinx. After all, the question of Antigone's *jouissance* is not resolved at the end of the piece. The Greek sphinx from the beginning—the Oedipus-Sphinx couple—is transformed into the Oedipus-Antigone couple. This is why Lacan always put the projectors on Antigone in his seminar on *Ethics*. Because she is the remainder of the whole operation: Isn't there something in her that the Sphinx incarnated earlier, in the aforementioned moment: the interrogation of feminine *jouissance*?

Lacan takes this up again in the following phrase: "[...] you will be able even toward evening to make yourself the equal of Tiresias, and like him, from having made the Other, to divine what I have said to you." Basically, the feminine hand that helps him—that can just as easily destroy him—is also the hand that can transform him into the equal of Tiresias, or, in other words, castrate him. When a man is made the equal of Tiresias, he is transformed into a woman. And after the littleman is made the Other, she can permit him to divine what was said.

What was said? It is that the voice of the feminine superego, the utterances that represent it, originate in her own *jouissance*, in her Other *jouissance* that is her own.

Lacan conceived of this demand of *jouissance* as a demand of the superego.

We know that, for Lacan, the superego forms an order of *jouissance*. The superego commands: "*Jouis*," to which one can only respond: "I understand." It is important to rid ourselves of the notion that the superego serves a prohibitory function. The idea that the superego pushes toward crime is not evident for those unacquainted with Lacan's work. It would have been difficult, for instance, to explain to the protestors of 1968—who proclaimed: "*jouir* without inhibition and without wasted time"—that, in truth, they were merely miming the superego's commandment. The protestors thought they were the most libertarian group in existence; they believed they had overcome all social prejudices. To counter the social prohibition against *jouissance*, they proclaimed that we should "*jouir* over and over again," or, in other words, that we should "move toward death." *L'éthique de la psychanalyse*[3] was necessary to perceive that there was not a prohibition at the core of Freud's discovery of the superego but a scandal. The scandal of the Freudian discovery is that, whatever the layout of the world, *jouissance* is always driven beyond the pleasure principle. Those who advance in this space of *jouissance* without barriers soon find themselves in a state of horror. For this reason, the innocent voice that says "You satisfied me" should be qualified as belonging to the superego.

The following formulation signifies this very well: "the superegohalf (*surmoitié*) that does not superego as easily as the universal conscience." In other words, every man must confront this type of siren's voice. The voice of the sirens, which Ulysses rightfully distrusted, says the following: "Become a friend of women, do as Tiresias did. To truly understand them, you must make yourself a woman; try to approach the Other *jouissance*." The character of the superego that Lacan introduces in this passage seems amusing. But it is actually very serious. All of psychoanalysis, especially the post-Freudian current, is preoccupied with the distinction between the paternal and maternal superegos. Melanie Klein[4] contributed a great deal to the idea that the paternal superego, which so annoyed Freud in *Moses and Monotheism*, wasn't actually so terrible. It was the good, brave paternal prohibition, and it was no longer feared by anyone in a world turned upside down by the permissiveness that followed the two world wars, a world where education became radically permissive. What we have seen take shape, however, is more formidable: the maternal prohibition, the maternal superego. Hence the consideration of bad mothers, mothers that, like the Indians in the first westerns, were always necessarily evil. And this maternal superego creates difficulties far more serious than the paternal prohibition.

This is why the voice states: "reduce yourself to the dead father, let yourself be taken by the hand of Antigone"—Lacan says precisely "Thanks to the hand that will respond to you, insofar as Antigone you call it," that is to say: "Make yourself like Tiresias, the castrated lover."

There are two ways to make oneself like Tiresias. One good and one bad. And the psychoanalyst has a position to occupy in the feminist debate around this choice.

The misguided way to make oneself like Tiresias is

to want to be a friend, pretending to be beyond the phallic measure. It is also, without a doubt, misguided when men and women whisper secretly that they are the same, that nothing truly distinguishes them. Since the feminist debate found a way to root itself durably in the cultural tissue of Occidental civilizations, women beg men to spare them their constructions regarding the feminine mystery, claiming that they get on among themselves just fine. Men, they think, have enough issues to deal with on their own turf to be occupied with women's *jouissance*. The point of this debate, embodied by Madame Badinter[5] and by others, is that when it is clear that the man and woman's position is strictly definable in juridical terms—after all, one can speak about the use of *jouissance* quite well in terms of right—and that the struggle is being fought in the name of equal rights, there is no reason why we would not arrive at systemic equality: the one is the other and the other is one. From this equality, the deleterious power of the call to the Other *jouissance* could disappear like a mirage. According to this thesis, there would be a juridical way in which to make oneself like Tiresias. From this perspective, it would be possible to construct a legal system such that, beyond the status of the protective father, responsibilities for caring for children would be shared equally. Such equality of rights would extend to equality of *jouissance*.

Does psychoanalysis offer a new perspective in the debate? The conservative position would consider defending the idea that the feminine mystery will remain definitively mysterious and that, consequently, it is useless to believe in this method of distributing rights and responsibilities.

Psychoanalysis does not denounce the efforts in the struggle for equal rights as vain. It does not wish to discourage anyone. Psychoanalysis's position consists, rather, in maintaining that the voice of the superego, the deadly imperative, is only deadly for those who refuse to face the originality of the feminine position. It is only deadly for those who deny the specific origin of the feminine utterance, for those who deny the direct impact of the Other. In this regard, Bernini's *Saint Theresa* captures her embrace with the dead father, but, in another sense, it also expresses the *jouissance* of the Other whose presence is certain though nameless. The quiet utterance: "You satisfied me, littleman"—if it emanates from the superego, if it is indeed terrible—it is because the temptation to tear away at imposed limits finds its source here, beyond phallocentrism.

The position of the modern subject, which Lacan invites us to occupy, is certainly not to attach oneself to the mast of a ship, like Ulysses, nor to attach oneself to the phallic semblant in the manner of the Catholic Church. The Church maintains firm control over the direction of its ship by refusing modernity's discreet invitations, when the Pope, for instance, decides to bar women's access to the priesthood. The Catholic Church holds on stubbornly to the past because it is a grand defender of the phallic semblant. The issue here is not Jewish patriarchy, which is another matter entirely. The issue is rather its relation to the semblant. The Catholic priest is a man who, by renouncing the exercise of his organ, truly becomes a symbol. The Fathers of the Church really stumbled upon a brilliant idea with this very carefully planned practice. The conservative relation to modernity is much more careful than the liberal approach, which would consist in radically and rapidly modernizing the Church, leaving it thoroughly mixed up with overturned dogmas. And this could not happen without causing serious damage.

Things are different in religions that worship the mother goddess. Some might also be nostalgic for this epoch: "How great it was when *jouissance* was permitted." It is enough to reread *The Golden Ass* to get a realistic idea of the issue. There were always more males devoted to the mother goddess, all of whom were so committed that they castrated themselves one after the other. The religion of the mother goddess is above all a procession of disciples who castrate themselves.

We knew this during the nascent period of the Catholic Church as well. We can recall that there was a whole movement that promoted castration with enthusiasm. It was really about demonstrating just how far one was willing to go for the symbol. A lot of people wanted to castrate themselves. It became necessary to ban this practice and to oppose castration as practiced by the priests of Cybele to the symbolic castration of the vow of chastity. And it was equally necessary to distinguish between castration and circumcision. Saint Paul insisted on the "circumcision of the heart" over physical circumcision, thereby evoking Jeremiah's castigations: "Rid yourself of the foreskin of the heart."

Psychoanalysis opposes itself to the logic of the Catholic Church, a logic that promotes the phallic semblant. The path of psychoanalysis is not one of semblants; neither the semblant of the father nor the phallus. Its path, rather, consists of mobilizing all the resources of the said and of interpretation to point out that the Sphinx's words only have moral power if we ignore the necessity of facing it as sexuated beings. Or, in other words, in a world that represses castration, that denies or forecloses it, we, as analysts, will deal with the call of "obscure gods"—this is the term Lacan uses at the end of Seminar XI[6]—or, to put it another way, the subject will know to recognize this call of the gods as the call of woman.

Lacan's ethical revolution in psychoanalysis was to show that, if the superego is dangerous, it is not because it prohibits, but because it pushes toward crime. It pushes us to *jouir.* Lacan shows no complacency toward these injunctions to "*jouir* more" that enchanted the end of the '60s. The general idea he develops is that we *jouit* too much and do not desire enough. To *jouir* does not take a lot of effort. In this regard, the human being, the subject, Lacan says, is content[7]; he has had more than his proper dose. Today, the subject wants to add *jouissance* to the world without limit—like the pervert who absolutely wants to make *jouir*, who pushes back the bounds of the brave neurotic's *jouissance*.

The superego pushes toward crime and, here, the voice of "superegohalf"[8] is the veritable superego. Not the maternal superego, which really isn't the worst, but the feminine superego insofar as it pushes toward a particular crime: "make yourself the equal of Tiresias!" Here is a "superegohalf that doesn't superego[9] as easily as the universal conscience." This universal conscience is considered, from time to time, as constitutive of the superego in psychoanalysis. The voice of conscience is not universal; it is particular for each subject, it announces itself in a particular register for everyone. As such, it is the opposite of universal conscience.

There is, then, this voice that invites the littleman to "make himself the equal of Tiresias." But Lacan does not invite the littleman to what he surrenders to this imperative. He invites him, rather, to what is "refuted, made inconsistent, indemonstrable, and undecided" by the feminine superego.

These verbs—*s'inconsister, s'indémontrer, s'indécider*—which are not used widely in the French language, especially when they are used reflexively, refer to the three registers of inconsistency, the indemonstrable, and the undecidable. These three verbs are all forms of the incompleteness found in Gödel's theorem, which demonstrates that, whatever the system, there will always be, at one and the same time, propositions that are both true and indemonstrable, a fact which poses the problem of the decidable and problems linked to consistency. Consequently, these three verbs are all ways of saying the S(Ⱥ).

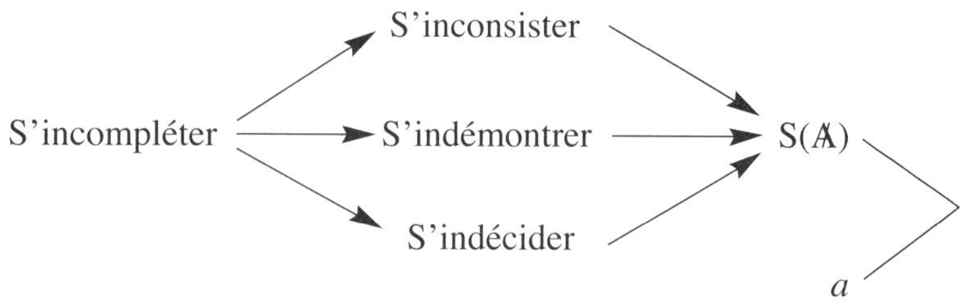

The prefix "in," in French, is privative. And, in this phrase, Lacan shows that, when one is on the male side—and this can include women themselves—the true service one can offer to the Sphinx is to not make oneself the friend of women, but to restore one's relationship to $S(\not{A})$, the relation to inconsistency, to undecidability, the relation to the lack in the Other. Here, man can make himself "the intermediary through which woman becomes Other for herself just as she is Other for him." It would also be, here as elsewhere, a mistake to want to be the Other of a subject, and, in essence, to transfer this call to the voice of the sirens: "Come and join me, then you will be my other."

When faced with the superego, how can one refute its word, make it inconsistent, indemonstratable, undecidable? From its words, "from what ex-sists of the paths of its *dire*." What does "the paths of its *dire*" signify? The demand of the feminine subject is a demand of *jouissance*, but of a *jouissance* distinct from the phallic modality. The ways of feminine words originate beyond penis envy (*penisneid*). It begins with "You satisfied me." On the "feminine" side of the formulas of sexuation, we rediscover the two directions with which the feminine subject has a relation. On one side, the point of inconsistency in the Other and, on the other, *jouissance* or the *plus-de-jouir*. To respond to the superego, it is necessary to decode and divine the *jouissance* from which the menacing *jouissance* originates, this siren's voice that commands: "Make yourself my Other!" And one must respond: "There is no Other of the Other." Just as when one hears the call to "be everything for me as I'm everything for you," one must remind the feminine subject that there is no speech that satisfies this demand for totality. We must start with this *jouissance*, as it can speak itself. Which is what inspires Lacan to write: "from what ex-sists." It is necessary that a minimum ex-sists for sense where a minimum displacement is required to have access to the paths of its *dire*. From here the utterances of demand will be returned to the point where "there is no Other of the Other" $S(\not{A})$. This is the place Lacan assigned to the analyst, the new Oedipus. Because it is no longer about revealing his place with regard to man, or to identify him with the Phallus, but to know how to respond to this call.

This is why the following paragraph states:

> Whence the analyst from another source than this Other, the Other of my graph [...] and signified by S of A barred: *notall*, from where would he know how to find fault in what abounds from the pettifogging logic by which the relation to sex goes astray, in wanting that its ways lead to the other half?[10]

This passage also merits a slow reading. And I will read slowly, but, put simply, I want to underscore that, to read this page carefully, we cannot say that Lacan assigned the analyst to the woman's position. There is no feminization of psychoanalysts, nor encouragement for us all to become like Tiresias. Lacan expects the psychoanalyst to know how to respond to the feminine superego. The analyst can return the feminine superego to the true logic of the feminine position, which is to denounce the semblants that aim to create consistency in the Other. It is incumbent upon the analyst to be the one who says: "You want there to be this Other that exists for you? Recall that there is no Other of the Other, and that the last word always escapes." In language, there is this point that always eludes us that we, as psychoanalysts, must deal with. Some women are able to show how one can have the closest connection with this point while creating the paths for saying something from a point of certitude.

Here, Lacan hitches psychoanalysis to a task where it is no longer necessary to endorse the fiction that there is a happy and systemic relation between the sexes, which are split into two halves. Humanity's division into two halves according to sex remains a complicated and inexplicable phenomenon. What exactly sets the sex ratio? This question is the object of a study that greatly progressed since the research on DNA, and the scientific world hopes that the study of the human genome can finally deliver us some additional insights. But for now the question remains open and has not been mastered. Which is fortunate, in some ways. Entire civilizations have, in effect, tried to master the rate of reproduction by, for example, killing girls at birth—which is something the Chinese have become very specialized in. There is even an entire section of the sciences of feminine demographics that calculates the number of girls assassinated at birth, based on parameters such as fertility rates and population census data. The results permit, not by genetic manipulation, but by radical manipulations, the adjustment and maintenance of a stable rate of reproduction in these societies. Many societies have tried to correct the strange symmetry of the sex ratio.

The prejudice that for every man there is a woman relies, in large part, on this biological contingency—which surely constitutes an interesting factor in the maintenance of the species—but that, beyond symmetry, suggests that there are, rather, two halves plus the superego. There are the two halves of humanity that are distributed by the phallus with the question of the imaginary organ marked in one of the two halves. In effect, the phallus distributes the two halves of humanity, but there is still something left over—namely, the superegohalf (*surmoitié*), that must be situated beyond the phallus and that takes on most of the burden.

This call to *jouissance* is of considerable importance for psychoanalysis. If one has forgotten it, one should recall the most familiar representation of the psychoanalyst, i.e. the priest of the ritual of castration, or, even better, the exegete of phallic *jouissance*. The psychoanalyst would then explain that everything in the world has a sexual meaning. Without him, this is what is taught in the *salles de garde*. But it is also what serves advertising and industry, which want to offer us serialized sexual dreams. And to accomplish this, it is necessary for them to render the object desirable. There is a whole industry that makes incredible profits by selling the object, an industry that a whole universe of financiers has tapped into. Whole sectors of industry and science hold on exclusively to the idea of the phallic distribution of the world and *jouis-sens*. It is an idea that works in a convincing and demonstrable fashion.

And this is what psychoanalysis could be. The voice that explains to the world that what guides it, the compass that orients it, is phallic distribution.

Lacan recommends refraining from abounding in sexual sense. He claims that modern man, contemporary man of the industrial era and of the ethics of scientific truth, is encumbered with sexual matters. To abound in the symbolic and sexual sense, bathe in it, makes modern man a being who is much more helpless than man of the classical age.

Lacan noted that the charm of classical novels, novels that therefore precede the epistemological cut, is that the man of sin was handling complicated sexual matters with much greater ease. When one sees the shame of political leaders getting caught red-handed with another man or woman, when one sees the whole affair this incites, with all the moral injunctions concerning their comportment and the advice to devote themselves to their families, then we can truly measure the distance between us and the 17th century, organized around the court of the king, and the 18th century, which was libertine. Read the *Mémoires* of l'Abbé de Choisy.[11] Though the ladies were jealous of the slightly-too-bronze robes he wore to collect alms in his church and though he was asked to stay away from scandal—and to adopt a more modest outfit—no one ever asked him to dress like a man. The king's brother's homosexuality was notorious and never turned the world upside down. The king had his court, he had his sweeties, and each one calculated how to seduce the lover of the moment to gain access to coveted posts; all of this was built into the calculus of the world.

The actual discontent in civilization depends on the use civilization makes of psychoanalysis. Psychoanalysis has contributed to ambient permissiveness, but the world is nevertheless still burdened by sex and the relationship to the inequality of the distribution of *jouissance*. Permissiveness in cultural values has actually made it possible to have a sort of exalted representation of evil—a term Lacan used. And this has permitted the exaltation of extremist perverse forms. A certain usage of psychoanalysis that intended to relieve the world of the superego's call has only harmed the discourse.

It can be seen very clearly in Mia Farrow and Woody Allen's experience. The whole family was in analysis and diverse types of therapy. Woody Allen himself has been going for more than thirty years. Having surprised himself with his wife's adopted daughter, he commented on the matter with these words: "We are using this experience to deepen our relationship." The American journalist who wrote about the breaking news wrote: "Who will win? What is certain is that the losers are the psychologists, the American shrinks, the 'head reducers.'" Allen, however, saw it differently: "That a family uses specialists for as many years as we have and still ends up in the mess we are in says nothing about the profession." Ten years later, moreover, all of this was forgotten thanks to *Everyone Says I Love You*.[12]

The difficulty of the call to the superego is not diminished by practices of appeasement or by that which, in the relation of the couple, presents itself as the ideal of temperance. In the end, this small fact testifies less to a therapeutic failure than it demonstrates that either one does not pull back when confronted by $S(\not{A})$—and instead strives, endeavors to disprove, make inconsistent, indemonstrable and undecidable—or one becomes a prisoner condemned to fussing over sex, caught by this call to the voice of the sirens.

In the whole affair, psychoanalysis can do nothing but give value to and underscore the dimension of the act in Mia Farrow's reasoning. This story teaches us that psychoanalysis does not have a preventative effect. Melanie Klein, however, conceived of psychoanalysis in exactly these pre-emptive terms. And she was not the only one. It is also a strategy of rendering psychoanalysis acceptable to the political master. If it can first and foremost alleviate suffering, like fluorine in water prevents cavities, then what solace! Winnicott responded that Kleinian prevention seemed naïve because, as he put it, the effect of psychoanalysis in education permits a much greater permissiveness and expression of drives, in particular the death drive. Permissiveness spreads but does not pose an obstacle to suicidal temptations. The death drive constitutes a limit to the hope of totally overcoming unhappiness.

Psychoanalysis is not as optimistic as modern medicine, which predicts the end of depression. Statistics, however, indicate that the consumption of psychotropes shows no sign of slowing down in any part of the world. With this data available, one must realize that the enthusiastic call of the sciences does not live up to its promises. How, after all these years of continuous victory, have we arrived at such a level of psychotropic consumption?

Lacan gives us a response. Of course the death drive cannot be diminished, but he also indicates that, although the psychoanalytic operation begins by valuing phallic sense—which is, in fact, the true lever of our operation, the lever by which we find an incidence in the symptom—it is really about waiting for the point beyond sense. By valuing phallic sense, we leave a remainder, we leave the aforementioned superegohalf (*surmoitié*) without affronting it. This is why Lacan can say that, beyond interpretation, he places the highest value on discourse without speech (*discours sans parole*). It is about trying to account for the deception of unveiling the impasses of sex, the impasses that are unique to the human species.

1. Lacan, J., "L'Étourdit," op. cit., p. 468.
2. Lacan, J., Seminar XXI, *Les non-dupes errent*, (1973-1974), lesson of January 15, 1974. Unpublished.
3. Lacan, J. Seminar VII, *L'éthique de la psychanalyse,* (1959-1960), Paris, Le Seuil, 1986..
4. Klein, Mélanie, *La psychanalyse des enfants,* Paris, Puf, 1969.
5. Badinter, Elisabeth, *L'un est l'autre ; des relations entre hommes et femmes,* Paris, Odile Jacob, 2002.
6. Lacan, J., Seminar XI, *The Four Fundamental Concepts of Psychoanalysis,* 1964, Norton, USA.
7. Lacan, J., *Télévision*, 1974,
8. "*sur-moitié*": a pun referring to a superego (*sur-moi*) that is the better half (*moitié*) of man; a feminine superego.
9. "*surmoite*": a play on words between *surmonter* (to overcome) and *avoir les mains moites* (to have sweaty palms).
10. Lacan, J., "L'Étourdit," op. cit., p. 468.
11. Choisy, Abbé de, Memoirs: *Mémoires pour servir à l'histoire de Louis XIV, par feu M. l'abbé de Choisy, suivis de Mémoires de l'abbé de Choisy habillé en femme*, edited and annotated by Georges Mongredien, Paris, Mercure de France, 2000, Collection: Le temps retrouvé.
12. *Everyone Says I Love You*: 1996—US—Musical Comedy Romance—1h41. Director: Woody Allen. Actors: Natalie Portman, Tim Roth, Julia Roberts, Edward Norton, Goldie Hawn, Lukas Haas, Drew Barrymore, Woody Allen, Alan Alda. Writer: Woody Allen.

Moments in a Love Story

MARIE HÉLÈNE BROUSSE

translated by ASUNCIÓN ALVAREZ

The experience of analysis, unlike the demand for psychotherapeutic help, is characterized by a belief, the belief that there exists a truth, a truth which is hidden, which escapes us. This truth is placed by neurotics in a causal position as the cause of their symptom, the cause of their suffering, of their malaise... They outwit it, they seek it where it is not, convinced that knowledge of the truth will transform what "is not working" into something that "works." The love of truth is thus at the start of every analysis, together with the desire to know.

In psychosis, the subject arrives with a truth which he does not believe in, given that he is certain of it this truth that inhabits him, that arranges the world according to an unbreakable logic.

Thus we can deduce that truth is the mode of access to knowledge for every speaking subject. We can also think that truth constitutes the libidinal face of knowledge, the face of knowledge related to the drive, to the structure of speech. But we can move on to writing—I mean, mathematical writing—in order to erase the link between knowledge and truth, or, more precisely, to remove its satisfaction aspect from truth, to detach it from meaning, as stressed by Lacan. Thus it is reduced to the binary opposition of truth and falsity.[1]

Our subject-supposed-to-know involves another definition of knowledge. For simplicity's sake, and from the analysand's point of view, we can certainly, take the subject-supposed-to-know to be incarnated by the analyst who is allowed by his position to claim a certain knowledge of the unconscious and its muddles; or, from the analyst's point of view, we can take the subject-supposed -to-know to unfold in the analysand's free association—we can even regard the chain of words constituted by both the analysand's utterances and the analyst's sayings as the subject-supposed-to-know. None of this is false. But it seems to me that this is not the core of the problem, as this doesn't necessarily affect the way in which knowledge is glued to truth; that is to say, it doesn't affect the libidinal charge of the signifying chain, the non-existent relation between a signifier and the thing whose truth it provides—which, for the speaking subject, arises from the sexual meaning, the meaning given by thc sexual relationship.

I will use elements taken from a cure to illustrate what I am saying. The conditions of an analysand's sex life constitute a symptom for him and he complains about them. Another side of his discourse shows him as devoted to the other's satisfaction, the only thing he believes he can do not to be abandoned. During the course of his work in analysis, he seeks in the data of his history—the particularities of the bond with his parents, their modes of *jouissance*—the knowledge, produced by the truth effect, which can transform this symptom. He brings things into relation, interrogates their structure, seeks to reduce this discourse which remains focused on the hardships of sex life to the signifying chain. Until a new element appears to the analyst, which had nonetheless been present from the beginning of the cure: however desperate or anxious the patient is or claims to be, his speech is nonetheless characterized by a jokiness, a comical character which is experienced and displayed in the cure. But not only this—the subject *jouit* the reputation of being the soul of every party, a clown, in his social life. This certainly fits in with his preoccupation for satisfying the other. A satisfaction that is acted out in the analytic link, a modality of constitution of the subject-supposed-to-know that is completely different from the expected and supposed knowledge found in the pattern of his history, in the signifying chain, in the unconscious which is supposed to be decipherable—his comical nature is at the crossroads of his stealthy sexual encounters and his daily malaise, as well as his analytic sessions. His comical nature is the other face of "what doesn't work." This face of the unconscious, acted out in transference in order to short-circuit the discourse on the search for truth as a decipherable meaning, should be privileged.

Jacques-Alain Miller, a long time ago, showed the difference between supposed knowledge and exposed knowledge. Thus I will not go back to this. The knowledge built by a subject on the signifying chain that constituted him, on the basis of non-erasable utterances and *lalangue* elements, ceases to be supposed and changes modality. Thus, in accounts of the pass, subjects try to expose it. Several elements take part in this change of modality of knowledge.

Firstly, belief: no more faith in the unconscious; it ceases to be placed in a causal position to support a truth which was actually not based on anything in the order of meaning and need, but only on *jouissance*. Following Jacques-Alain Miller's work on the last Lacan we might see, in the end of the belief in the unconscious-supposed-to-be decipherable and the rise of the fictional status of truth, the roots of the disenchantment with psychoanalysis and of this sadness which Lacan describes as being far from incompatible with enthusiasm—that is to say, with desire and with that which accompanies the passage toward becoming an analyst and the end of the cure. The unconscious becomes a kind of knowledge in the real, a knowledge which has no subject. It is constituted of sayings, earworms heard and engraved. This modification of belief actually arises from the passage from speech, its power, its value, to non-speech, the gibberish aspect of human words, even of those which have acted as a foundational axiom for our *jouissance* as speaking beings.

An analysand recently reduced his parents' recurring sayings to two formulas, the maternal and the paternal: "It would be better to be dead" and "Full retreat." Unveiling his parent's positions of *jouissance,* these utterances remain incarnated in him under the form of an absurd and yet irradiating knot, down to the least of his intimate thoughts, determining the color of the world in which he lives, against all rationality. This is the cure that turns his life into a useless detour and leads all desire to the silence of the tomb. The meaning of life, the truth of all knowledge, when exposed in the words in which they originate, are reduced to gibberish and thus allow the object to be glimpsed where it was veiled by the sexual relationship: where the transcendence of truth was supposed-to-be, idiocy appears. This is the end of the transcendence of meaning and the correlative transformation of truth into flat contingencics. For this analysand, the parasitical status of desire thus exposed leads to sadness, and his world easily takes on an apocalyptic nature.

The second factor is the rise of a third element within the binary opposition of knowledge and truth: in the first example I gave, it was the comical element. But all accounts of the pass provide examples of this. This is *objet a.* In the case which I brought up, this object, the phallus, organizes the subject's speech, his relationship to the signifier, that is to say, to the Other, but also assigns the subject a place with regard to the others. In Seminar X, *Anxiety,* Lacan defines the phallus as the object that brings *jouissance* "into the Other." The subject is thus the irradiation effect of the chain spoken by this object: the comical element is here the acting out of this object in transference. In psychoanalysis, truth is reduced to knowledge of this immanence of *jouissance,* that is to say of the object, in speech. Thus there is no transcendence of truth in speech. Transference, in its aspect as love, is determined by this interference of the object in what is said. Lacan, in his seminar *Les non-dupes errent,* defined love as that which results from the impossibility of a sexual bond with the object. Its foundation is impossibility, and its means is contingency. Thus it is a kind of event which can only be produced in the defiles of the symbolic, it is something that is said. It is an effect of what is said in analysis.

The more unconscious knowledge becomes real, the more it ceases to be a subject, without ceasing to be supposed.

The analyst's position is thus regulated by transference: it must slip into the place defined by the mode of *jouissance* being acted out. This is how I regard the analyst in the position of *objet a.* But he doesn't take this position without desire. This desire is not a desire to decipher, that is to say, a desire to take part in this search for truth and meaning, as his own history as an analysand revealed to him the meaninglessness of non-speech at the same time as the real nature of signifiers. The analyst's desire is no longer determined by the knowledge-truth relationship, by the love affair between knowledge and truth. Love, the drive modality of transference, is no longer love of truth, and the analysand's belief is no longer linked to truth, not even to the truth of psychoanalysis. Knowing what to expect regarding the unconscious as true knowledge, regarding the hopes created by the Name-of-the-Father, having witnessed the contingency of the solutions found to lodge *jouissance* in the Other despite his non-existence, is the subject detached from belief? Surely from belief in an Other who knows, who wants, who demands, who desires, who loves. But in the seminar *Les non-dupes errent,* Lacan does not locate the analytic solution in the end of belief, that is to say, in the end of transference. The question is, he says, how to be duped in the right way. Duped by what? Duped by the real. This is a funny way of putting it. Instead of love of truth as deciphered, which Freud bears witness to in many ways (the clearest of which is his hunt for the Wolf Man's primal scene or even the stress he laid on Dora's love for her father, on hysterics' love for castration in general), instead of love of meaning, Lacan proposes love as a way of giving consistency to the real. The disjunction of knowledge and truth, whose link lies in the symbolic basis for truth that is the Name of the Father, makes a new link possible: that of knowledge of *jouissance* and of the real. Love is modified there—Lacan goes so far as to write *a-mur* ("non-wall," as a play on *amour,* "love"), along the same lines as *a-parole* ("non-speech"). This love does not consist in covering the object with a beautiful image, or in cancelling the difference between the signifier and the body.

It no longer requires the marriage of *jouissance* and meaning, with whatever value. Certainly the Name of the Father, or rather the Names-of-the-Father, arrange the subjects' world, but the compass keeps pointing, with or without the father, towards the real of the satisfaction that inhabits them down to the most intimate of their representations. I wonder whether the end of analysis amounts to:

1. Seeing that what leads speaking beings is the nonsensical object which, in its stupid and ineffable existence, materializes the link between the three string circles and is the cause of desire; seeing thus the fragility under the guise of love: being duped by the real would be this—"saying the event with no blurring," without the relationship provided by any meaning.
2. Or else, and this is not a matter of either/or:
   Choosing by an act (for example, the passage toward becoming an analyst, which is renewed in every intervention in directed cures) the real which leads to what "we risk our necks for in all this business."

1. Lacan, Seminar XXI *Les Non-dupe errent,* lecture January 8th 1974, unpublished.

Albert Herter, *There is no sexual relation*, black chalk on paper, 2011

Sigmar Polke, *Untitled*, 1964-68/90, gelatin silver print, 23.7 x 19.8 inches

The Child as Object

Pierre-Gilles Gueguen

translated by Asunción Alvarez

I was once amazed to see in Times Square an advertisement for the brand "Buy Buy Baby," displaying the photo of a chubby child lying with his arms spread eagled like a merry Christ in diapers. There was something crude about this picture representing the child as just another occasional support for the shopping excitement of his parents. Beyond the pun in the brand name, some truth was barely hidden and thus revealed.

How should we consider the status of children in a world in which, given technological progress (particularly biotechnology and communications), a child can appear to be a product for consumption, tailored and custom-fit, but also standardized, for its parents, an interchangeable object for parental fantasms? This is what is suggested by those cases in which the child was "programmed" by careful contraception or else born by artificial insemination, medically followed throughout pregnancy, has been the object of scientific intervention for its sex to correspond to the parents' request, etc...

There is no doubt that, given scientific advances and the fall of paternal ideals, there is nowadays an extension of the fantasms projected onto the child, and possibilities to realize them although we must not forget that, at least since psychoanalysis exists, the child has been regarded as one of the means by which parents can satisfy their narcissism. Freud, when describing the Child King, "His Majesty the Baby," only proved to be a keen observer of his times. The Countess de Ségur did not write about her "perfect little girls" yesterday, and the ideal childhood, put otherwise, "objectivized," as shown by the work of historians, has always been an object of representation for adults.

But we should acknowledge that non-programmed births, the fierce ban on abortion, and medical negligence also cause damage. Thus we must distinguish between the progress made possible by Science and the damage arising from its misuse. We will not bring up any nostalgic points here as they are useless.

However, what the excesses of the market civilization in which we are living bring home to us, and what can be difficult to face and which we maybe thus should remember, is that every child is also and always, to a certain extent—at least for the mother—an object of satisfaction. Everything that must take place for the child to attain the status of subject takes place within the margin—what Lacan calls "the margin of the exteriorization of *objet a*."

In order to develop this line from the point of view of children's psychoanalysis, Seminar *Encore* is essential. Indeed, it renews our perspective and enriches it by including Lacan's development of *jouissance* and love within the discoveries concerning the unconscious structured like a language.

In this regard the pathways through Lacan's work opened up by J-A Miller in his course *The Flight of Meaning* place a new and arresting stress on the fact that, when Lacan spoke about children (which, it must be said, was rarely), he always regarded them more in their status as objects of *jouissance*, the refuse of a desire aborted too early on, than under their aspect as subjects.

This does not render invalid the thesis, so rightly operative, by which the child in the psychoanalytical cure is fully a subject of language and speech, but the light thrown by this approach gives a different value to the cure with children, and particularly to the question of its boundaries.

Let us add that the content of these texts on children, written in the late '60s, was not something completely new for Lacan and that, in the *Écrits* for instance, we can find the trace of this perspective, already initiated, but which he fully developed later on. The Gide case is exemplary in this regard. J-A Miller has shown[1] how the articulation proposed by Lacan, which sought to bring the case out of the modalities of the psychiatric approach, was built to locate the child Gide in the three registers of love, *jouissance*, and desire. Each one of these three poles makes it possible to examine the consequences of the child's being caught in the family discourse and the way in which he became a sexed being as a function of the way in which his parents themselves transmitted love, desire and *jouissance* to him. Nonetheless we should note (particularly in the Gide case, in which the aunt plays an essential role) that not everything takes place in the field of the nuclear family, and that the "margin for exteriorization" can produce its effects following interventions from people other than the parents.

But the commentary on the Little Hans case given by Lacan in Seminar IV highlights how, even though the child at first sees the mother as an almighty, devouring Other, a separating construction is created by virtue of the analysis: a construction that does not lead to the impeccable realization of the Oedipus complex or the castration complex, but which leads, along the lines of the "rubber logic" that Lacan deciphers in Hans—in his transferential relationship with Freud—to the creation of a version of the phallus that was compatible with a relationship to the Other (of the Other sex).

Indeed, this is the true question for psychoanalysis: how the passage from the object of *jouissance* (especially for the maternal Other) to the love of the object (condition for love and object choice) takes place for a subject, a passage which—in both sexes—entails a passage from filial love to love of the Other. This is also a great topos of Classical drama and Greek and Latin tragedy. Thus, it is always the "birth of the Other" that is at stake, an expression that we will use here in a restricted sense, not to designate the register of the Symbolic but to refer to the Other as a sexed other, according to the Lacanian developments of the '70s.

Indeed, Lacan went from the "function and field of speech and language" (which essentially presents the techniques for the extrication of the unconscious and the subject in his relationship to the phallus) to the propositions in *Encore* and *L'Étourdit*, "a radical conjunction of the Lacanian *it speaks* and *it enjoys*."[2]

The elements of the problem could be brought together, following Miller's reading of Lacan, by means of three factors:

1st factor: The starting point consists in interrogating oneself in order to find out whether for Lacan the *apparole*, the apparatus of speech (or *jouis-sens*, the enjoyment-meaning) is truly compatible with the Other. This concept of the Other, I would like to remind you, is often reduced to the Other of desire, but, for Lacan in the '70s, it was understood as the Other of radical otherness, that is to say, the Other sex. But precisely, the solution given by Lacan is that speech does not introduce us radically to this otherness, and thus that all sexuality remains partially "autistic," which might be put otherwise by saying that every sexual satisfaction remains paired to one's own body.

We can immediately see that, particularly in children's psychoanalysis, the question of the passage from oneself to the Other is not a given, inasmuch as "the Spring awakening," that is to say, the subject's true access to the Other sex by means of the sexual relationship is missing from the picture. However, although we are not dealing with the sexual relationship as such, we must nonetheless take into account the dimension of love (by means of transference, for example).

And besides, although there is no access to the Other sex through the sexual relationship, there is no less *jouissance*, and there can certainly be love and desire for a sexed being other than one's parents. In any case, there is a major problem which every subject must deal with, which is the abandonment of the maternal libidinal love.

2nd factor: It consists in carefully distinguishing Freudian libido from the Lacanian concept of *jouissance*. Whereas for Freud libido is paired to the genitality that is supposed to "arrange libido according to the sex" by means of the Oedipus complex, the *jouissance* that Lacan talks about overflows sexuality. It is paired to the drives, and not to genitality. Indeed, it is something that we deal with in parental love (which Lacan calls maternal *jouissance* or *père-version*), and which is present in the foreground in children's psychoanalysis.

3rd factor: It is based on the fact that Lacan little by little restricted the concept of the Other by using it to designate the partner to whom the surmounting of the auto-erotic satisfaction is addressed in a sexed body's relationship with another sexed body. This is not exactly homomorphous to the developments concerning sexuality in the *Three Essays on Sexuality*. But, as the Other is not a given, there is no sexual relationship which might qualify as "natural" (except maybe, according to Lacan, that between mother and son, a terrible endogamy). Thus operators are required to enable the passage from the sameness of *jouissance* of the real (the continuum of the drive) to the discontinuous otherness of the sexed relationship which goes through the Other of demand and the defiles of the signifier.

Thus the subject must resort to fictions, to simulacra,[3] to break out of the narrow field of maternal *jouissance* if we posit, with Lacan, that the Other does not exist.

It is these fictions, these semblants, that weave the web

of the fantasm and isolate, cut up *jouissance* by endowing it with otherness. These fictions are three: the phallus, *objet a*, and love.

The phallic fiction introduces us to desire by means of lack and the signifier, the fiction *objet petit a* isolates a remainder, and love places this remainder in the place of the Other (who nonetheless does not exist), and thus makes Him exist purely by virtue of the signifier.

Every fictional register, however, only operates thanks to language (or more precisely, thanks to discourse), and displays its own modes of failure:

—the phallic fiction can remain masturbatory *jouissance* of the organ or turn into a neurotic symptom

—the abjectal fiction can become a trait in perversion (fetishism) or turn into sublimation

—even love can become courtly love or become mystical love.[4]

Thus love appears on the side of the relationship to the Other: it is even its purely signifying condition, which is why the true achievement of the sexed position is marked in girls by the possibility of being a woman rather than a mother, and for boys by the loss of what they do not have—even beyond copulation—bearing to become a father.[5]

Nonetheless, we must specify the sense in which we understand love, as it can also miss its mark, as we have pointed out. The demand for love which is in question here is not that for the love that consists in wishing to be loved and leads all too soon to narcissism, but rather to lovers' love. It is also love inasmuch as it is linked to sexuality, and more especially to sexuality with a partner of the other sex—differently according to each sex.[6] For this reason, children's psychoanalysis always stops at the point in which a verification must take place in an encounter. Does transference love, the supposition of knowledge linked to the child's transference to the analyst, allow a kind of filial love-hate relationship (*hainamoration*)? Does it entail the promise of an encounter with another sexed body? Every end of analysis with a child can only allow, on these points, a conjecture comparable to a probabilistic calculation, all the more so inasmuch as the perfection of the "Otherification" of *jouissance* by Love is never fully attained.[7]

Although I cannot exhaust the richness of the approach to children's psychoanalysis from the point of view of *objet a*, I would like to bring up two points which I believe are important:

1) Although the great analysts of his time, and particularly those who were interested in children's psychoanalysis, such as Balint or Mahler, supposed that there is an original, satisfactory love between child and mother, Lacan straightaway supported Melanie Klein's theses. That is to say, for him the relationships of imaginary aggressiveness and the question of *kakon* prevail. This was not simply a stage in Lacan's thought, but rather remained present throughout all his teaching, and if he was occasionally able to praise Winnicott, it was due to his conception of the transitional object, not because of his advice to mothers.

But in parallel he locates its place in maternal love. Let us notice that this is a place set apart, original in its way of locating love and in no way devalued.

If for Lacan there is indeed a "primordial relationship with the mother," it is a relationship of *jouissance* and satisfaction, not of love. Nonetheless, the mother progressively introduced "deprivation of needs by the very fact that they are satisfied," that is to say, that she contributes, through the satisfaction granted by her care, to introduce the relationship with the Other. However, "this privilege of the Other outlines the radical shape of the gift of what he does not have: his love."[8] Maternal love thus involves, like the love for the Other sex, a purely signifying operation which shows the child:
a) that it does not saturate the desire of the mother as an object of *jouissance* (the supposed perversity of the mother), but rather that it is the object of her love, that is to say, the referent of her orientation toward the Other.
b) that it is not reduced to the organ which she lacks, but beyond

and in its particularity, the child symbolizes her lack-in-being (-ϕ) and thus her desire even beyond the satisfaction of need. When this operation fails, we are dealing with two figures, that of the capturing mother or that of the abandoning mother—both of which figures can go so far as to generate psychosis.

Otherwise put, this means that the mother's position is deduced from the woman, and not that one becomes a woman by becoming a mother.

Let us insists on this point, which justifies Lacan when he talks about the child as giving the truth of the parental couple in its symptom (i.e. his definition of the child as symptom not only of the mother but of the parental couple): inasmuch as the mother and the father's relationship is not that of the love of a sexed body for a sexed body—otherwise put, is not regulated by castration and sustained by a pure operation of the signifier beyond the *jouissance*'s failure to make the sexual relationship exist—the child will suffer.

Thus "motherly love," in its usual sense, has various facets, its facets as failure: *jouissance* love, symptomatic love when love is reduced to wishing to be loved or when it is detached from the love for another sexed body.

Here the example provided by Gide is clearly illuminating. For his mother, the dimension of love seems to have been mostly homosexual (the governess), and something in the child was mortified which led him to have a single, demanding love for Madeleine, with no sexual realization. For Madame Gide, the dimension of desire was raised upon that of duty, and for this reason she transmitted this sadness to her son, as well as the exercise of a sexuality which was most often masturbatory.

2) Every child takes at first the place of a remainder, a piece of refuse originating in what failed in his parent's love relationship—every child "seals a union" and is its mark and product. For this reason, there is a real danger of the child's serving as the copula, the link between them, forever. Children's clinic shows many

examples of this (what we call, following Lacan: the child who is the mother's phallus, who is the phallus which the mother lacks).

What makes it possible for the child no longer to take this place is the construction of the fantasm in analysis. Analysis operates upon the fantasm, says Lacan: that is to say, it constructs the fictions, the semblants by which the child is able to spell out the object of its fantasm, that is to say the object that the child is for the Other.

In the register of desire, the child can access the fact that having a penis or not is not the essential question, as both sexes always lack the phallus.

With the support of love, the child can transform this lack, placing the object in question in this empty space. By virtue of the analytic transference, the empty place is restored to the child in which "the object of its fantasm" has a chance of being exteriorized—which is also the object that the child was for the Other.

1. (cf. the article "Le Gide de Lacan")
2. We are referring in particular to the lectures of January 31st and February 7th 1996. "La fuite du sense," unpublished course.
3. J-A Miller examines this question in his Seminar Eric Laurent "L'Autre qui n'existe pas et ses comités d'éthique" 1997-8 unpublished.
4. Cf. in particular Seminar XX p.48. J-A Miller notes in his course ("La fuite du sens," op. cit) that in these pages Lacan treats love and *jouissance* as a pair of opposites: enjoying substance leads toward the One, whereas Love corresponds to the very essence of the signifier in its effort toward the Other.
5. J-A Miller, June 96, Paper in the EEP Lausanne conference.
6. Cf. in particular J-A Miller, "Donc," unpublished lecture of May 11th 1994.
7. See in this sense the last pages in Seminar XI, in which Lacan talks about Spinoza's *amor intellectualis dei* in order to point out that Kant and Sade are more truthful, a passage commented upon by Miller in his 1990 course: "Le Banquet des analystes."
8. Lacan J. "La signification du phallus" *Écrits*, le Seuil, Paris 1966, p690.

Eating alone in the byways of Smithson

CATHY LEBOWITZ

Again I imagine taking the same trip. Putting the mirrors where he put them. Would I end up bruised next to the rented Dodge?

> Art critics are generally poets who have betrayed their art, and instead have tried to turn art into a matter of reasoned discourse, and occasionally, when their 'truth' breaks down, they resort to a poetic quote.
>
> Robert Smithson, "A Sedimentation of the Mind: Earth Projects," 1968

I painted at home as I moved from apartment to apartment. One apartment was on a street flanked by garbage trucks, another lined with police cars parked head first. I painted for eight years in an old East Village apartment facing an airshaft. Pigeons nested and cooed. I suspected a bordello on the second floor. Many men knocked, and when the door opened, the lights were low and women sat in bras. It was just for a while, after the tenant below me hit his head and rotted for ten days.

I learned to paint looking at still lifes. A teacher once said it takes ten years to learn how to paint. It was a productive place to experiment without knowing what I was doing.

I kept trying to paint Duccio's *Flight into Egypt*. The band of craggy mountains. The ocher desert. A woman in blue robes on a donkey being led by a man with a pale gray green torso, which I remember being bare. I wanted Duccio's recession. I wanted to find the plane of his mountaintops. Why do the mountains end so abruptly? How far apart are the trees?

A golden rectangle is defined by the proportion of its sides. If you divide the rectangle into a square and a new rectangle, the sides of the new rectangle will be in the same proportion as the original rectangle. Continue partitioning in this way until it is a whirling rectangle, which looks like this:

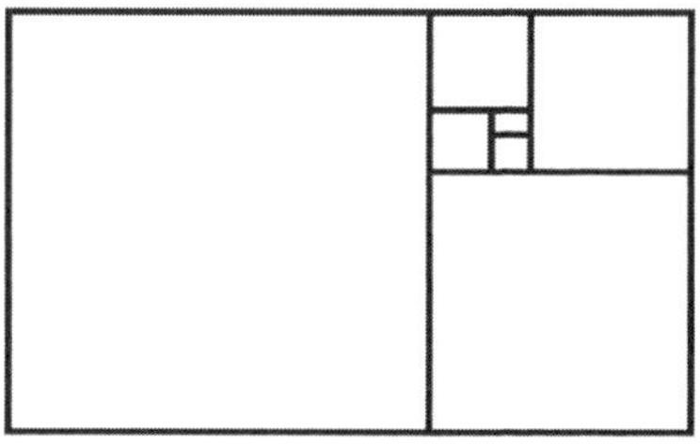

A whirling rectangle forms the architecture for a Fibonacci spiral, which looks like this:

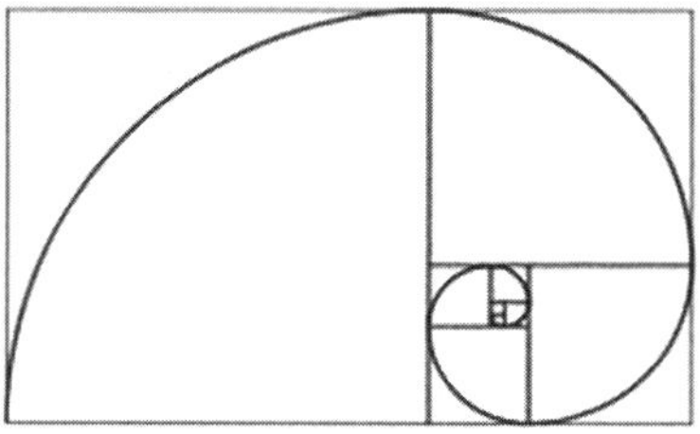

Eventually, the unconscious replaced still life. There was freedom in painting what no one could see.

I painted a tree and a girl in a long dress with a train and a veil. She hiked up her dress as she stormed away from the tree.

I painted a figure with the ghostly face of a knight. The upper body was splayed across a table and the lower body dissolved into a rhythm of intersecting rectangles. You might not recognize the knight. The painting was quite abstract. But to me, the knight was my mother. I painted other pictures of my mother, but none of them looked like her.

I painted a double portrait. The head on the right had round blue eyes with white centers, and looked like an embryonic Homer Simpson. The head on the left was fierce. A long nose and wide, fanged grin. Like she might eat her little son. This was Blue Balls and his mother.

I wrote about them on a manual typewriter, without thinking, just writing. If I didn't know what to type I wrote the same sentence again.

May 15, 1994
Blue Bals was verry close to hismothr. blue balls and his mother were very close. You could tell a lot about blue ball's mother from her dresses. blue balls was having hallucinations. the baby in the crib is a coversheet, a door. To learn more about blue balls i must fiind out more about his moter.

My Lacanian friend Josefina recently told me that I get upset about doors a lot. I once made her a flash animation of a dream I had of my father stealing the door to my apartment.

I made more paintings of Blue Balls. The lumpen pink figure stood in the upper right, looking down a light-filled hall. I wrote the blue words "A raking light fell across blue balls imagination." In the last painting of Blue Balls, the head was double-faced. In the area of his groin, folds of pink collected like a reef octopus. The unconscious is predictable.

The elegant curves of the pigeon's head and body flow into one another seamlessly. One afternoon, I was sitting on a stool in the studio looking at a painting. A pigeon landed on the open screenless windowsill. It started investigating, turning its head sideways, ducking and peeking its neck in increments through the window. Head turn, neck swoop, head turn, neck swoop. After some time of this, it stepped one red-orange foot over the threshold and then the other. It stepped onto the palette right in some paint, leaving behind yellow footprints.

I dreamed I was at the ATM on LaGuardia Place. Mark Rothko interrupted and told me I was done, even though I was in the middle. In the same dream, Philip Guston made me throw away a candle with a hairball stuck to it. Is this how the unconscious is structured like a language?

The last paintings I made were simple, awkward scenes—my version of Duccio's escape over and over. Most had craggy mountains and a field with trees or craters or brick enclosures, and sometimes the mouth of a cave. The figures were odd and naked, doing enigmatic things, like holding a crown shape over a hole in the ground, kneeling behind a tree and eating, sleeping behind a wall of bricks in a field of pylons. These I scanned into the computer and planned to make into a game where you click on a part of the picture and go to another scene.

Another
The rare phenomena of the Vardoger flies by: premonitory sight or sound of a person before the person arrives.

And another
If
i. The old split between art and science formed a fault through Ka like "the obstetric line seen on fruits"
then
ii. It kept her from wondering about the circumference, everywhere.
iii. The rear guard will linger to mend the fault.

Josefina and the Chesire Cat

I was walking with Josefina in Soho after dinner. She was talking about the essay she is writing for a magazine called

"Culture/Clinic." The name refers to Lacan's influence in society and in psychoanalysis. She has been talking about it for a while. She always starts with the Chesire cat. The slogan on the Culture/ Clinic's announcement is "we are all mad in here." These words Josefina has traced to Alice in Wonderland. The cat disappears, the mouth stays. The mouth is a "part body." The libido attaches to a part body. Josefina tells me.

She is trying to think of other examples of part bodies to include in her essay. She had seen the Brion Gysin show at the New Museum, where William Burroughs and Gysin's cut-ups were on display. In their text and picture collages, she saw a story about a boy; he disappears and the smell of burning leaves is left behind. The smell of burning leaves, she wants to call it the "part body."

I ask "What about Milos Forman's Loves of a Blonde. She cuts herself in pieces for him. You told me that." "I don't remember" Josefina said "Milos Forman, Milos Forman." "Yes, it was you, who else would have said that—'she cuts herself in pieces for him with *words*.'"

On the same ride to the Yucatan as Robert Smithson, I place mirrors where he did. The horizon comes under my car, the way it was always under his. The "smoking mirror" talks to me, tells me to remember that the camera is a portable tomb. The picture is in my eye but I am not in the picture.

VardØger (vard-deh-ay'-grr)
i. If she
thinks she is being followed,
ii. then she turns around
iii. but she
knows no one will be there.

Firebreather's parents are divorced. His mother wants him to live a normal life, but his father, a firebreathing dragon, wants his son to accompany him in his hijinx. Firebreather tries to fit in at school, but he does not.

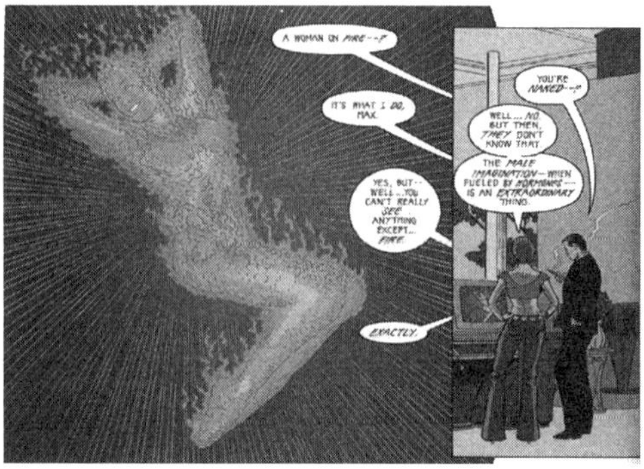

Beatriz Bonilla da Costa is the most prominent Brazilian superhero in the DC comic universe. Her codename is Fire, but she has also been known as Green Flame and Green Fury.

Josefina and the Hysteric

I went over to Josefina's. She told me about being an hysteric. The hysteric makes someone her master so that she can grab them and shake them against the wall and demand to know "Who am I?" That is Lacan's hysteric's discourse as I understand it from Josefina. It is one of four discourses: master, university and analyst are the other three. Lacan's four discourses mean very little to me when I read about them and look at the equations myself. But when Josefina tells me about the master's discourse and the hysteric's discourse, which she does quite often, she makes them seem alive, and relevant. I can see my actions, my complaints, according to this structure. "Can I stop making people into masters?" I ask her. "Deal with it," she says, "deal with what you are doing." "Why do I do it?" I ask her. "That is not a question that can be answered," she says. And I want to shake her and demand to know why I do it, and I see I have made her the master.

Ka finds soft spots. Her silky silicon device lights up when the field becomes irregular. Walking under the Williamsburg Bridge on Columbia Street, near the stray cats, she felt the atmosphere thicken for a moment. She took out the compass and in its hemisphere read the static. The increase in density extended no wider than her body. She stepped back and forth across the spot. She pushed hard against it, but it adapted to accommodate her seamlessly. She ripped at it with a blade, but the surface maintained its integrity. She stood still in the spot for two days but nothing happened.

The essay "Incidents of Mirror-Travel in the Yucatan" (1969) maps a drive that is an artwork. Smithson rents a pickup truck and arranges twelves square mirrors on the ground at nine locations. He takes a photograph of each "mirror displacement." His narrative comes complete with visitations from Tezcatlipoca. The Aztec deity lost a foot in battle with an earth monster, and an obsidian mirror grew in place of the foot.

Ka finally tells her: I know you are on fire, but the job requires embers too.

For Vardoger, it was all movement to an experimental hypothesis.

Josefina and the Confines of Sex

Josefina says there is one way to make love. The way you do it is: The man stays still and hard inside the woman, and the woman, also still, contracts and relaxes her muscles around the penis. Eventually, deep inside, the cervix will pulsate strongly and involuntarily, over and over, around the man's penis, until he ejaculates. This is the only way to make love, according to Josefina.

Ka went to the beach and looked for the tin can that would look back at her. She went to the hotel room to gaze out the window, hoping to see herself among the lights of the city.

Ka stood in the dark behind the vault. She knew the rake was in there, she could hear his thoughts. Ruined interference. With the rake, it's always disruption.

Smithson maps the mind onto the earth by setting words in poetic relation: glacial reveries, mental rivers, cliffs of thought undermined by brain waves. Like the earth, the mind is in a constant state of erosion. In his essay "A Sedimentation of the Mind," his comparisons and conflations repeatedly draw attention to a surface invaded by crevices. It becomes an ideology. "Words and rocks contain a language that follows a syntax of splits and ruptures." Like Lacan's unconscious, Smithson's words and rocks are structured like a language.

Josefina and Matthew Barney's *Cremaster*

We started doing interviews. Maybe we found it hard to write. I really wanted to know and she was always ready to answer questions about Lacan. She said I seemed more overwhelmed by the theory than most people. She was happy with our interviews and she published one in every issue. I got mad when she'd rewrite her answers after I'd asked the questions.

> Cathy Lebowitz: I have a lot of questions about Matthew Barney's *Cremaster*. Do you have a Lacanian interpretation of the films?
>
> Josefina Ayerza: Not an immediate one. Let's see. The allegory in *Cremaster* seems to come before the word—

like in dreams. Dreams do not exist before you tell the dream... We have though this one word: *cremaster*. I hear it addresses the muscle which raises and lowers the testicles.

CL: But Lacan theorized the stain in the work of art and the relation between the screen and the viewer. Don't these ideas come into play with Matthew Barney or any visual art work. Most visual art doesn't include words directly. Did Lacan dismiss art (without words directly placed on the screen) as imaginary, as that which does not exist?

JA: As a work of art Matthew Barney's *Cremaster* is using the structure of language—it goes over and above the symbolic even if it doesn't do so with words. In the case of Robert Gober, for instance, the words on the Pedigree bag instructing you to open it and feed the cat—have certainly lost their meaning. However the fact that art is structured doesn't add up to its existence. Art does not exist, what exists are works of art—in that they come forth one by one.

CL: Yes I see. But it is not only the artist that can supply the words. In Lacanian analysis, even, the analyst's words are considered fair game for interpretation. So the words I speak about Barney's work could be used as the "dream spoken." He supplies the dreams, I supply the words. Do you agree?

JA: I agree. Tell me...

CL: I was thinking about this scene in *Cremaster 3*. He

gets his teeth knocked out and is put in a dentist chair. The men attach a rubberish sheet to his face leaving his mouth open. Quite awful looking his gums exposed. And as they stand around him they look at his genitals; he is naked I think. And his genitals are a bizarrely shaped round thing, which looks like a gas cap on a car, intricate though, like a round seashell with symmetrical hornlike forms. It's outside the body like a man but not at all like a penis. Even the men are quite shocked by it, or they are disgusted by it. Then Richard Serra comes in and inserts a metal form in his mouth. This metal form is the result of the resurrected Gary Gilmore's body that has been placed in a car and smashed relentlessly by 6 cars, until it is this kernel—it reminded me of Zizek by way of Lacan, the kernel of the real. The thing that is left, the surplus. Anyway, Serra inserts this thing in Barney's mouth and presses into his exposed tissue, the gums and stuff being held open by the rubber sheet. And as he does this, a soft long sack emerges from Barney's rectum. And from the sack emerges a row of teeth. Teeth like the one's he had knocked out? And pink gooey liquid surrounds it and drips through a crack in the table/chair he is on. The teeth also slide down and they begin to loose their form. And gel together into a long white solid form. It is the strangest thing. The men who are disgusted by the thing coming out of his rectum eventually leave him alone in the room. And the teeth keep joining into this one tube, or rod. What has passed from the mouth has come out of his

> ass and reformed into formlessness. They took his teeth so he can be given this metal kernel of the real. This is his passage through a stage of the Masons, from one kind of apprentice to another higher level.

I try to imagine a device that grows in the human body sensitive to electromagnetic waves. With the bird, it is an enervated region of the beak. When it fails, cues are mistaken for permanent landmarks.

Witnesses saw me arrive. I didn't say "how was your day?" I just walked up the stairs.

I always take notes.

Ka's scenarios of failure multiply:

I am told to lie down and stay still.
I want to sit up...I won't..........
......I want to sit up......I won't......
................I want to sit up......
I feel sick......I sit up.

Red fourteen-sided sculptures overrun the apartment. She started making them from long pipe cleaners and thin jewelry wire after the Buckminster Fuller show. They are called

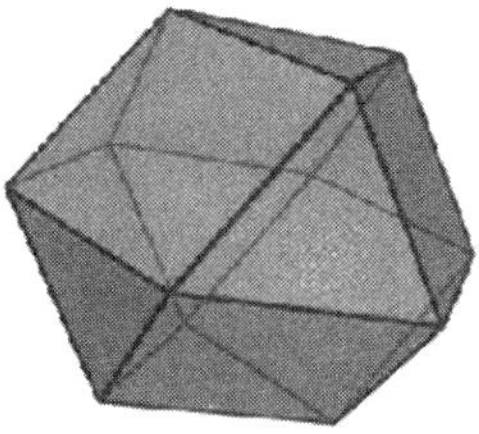

tetradecahedrons, and of the many possible tetradecahedrons, her red ones are truncated octahedrons. The fourteen faces consist of six squares and eight triangles. She only had to join six squares, and the triangles came along.

Ka's muscleless lover took her to the Marriot. She rode an elevator forty flights to get to the lobby. He did not want a room. He wanted to leave her there at the spinning bar overlooking the neon.

I had dinner with Josefina on Friday before she leaves for some months. I drank a glass and a half of wine while we talked. She kept talking about the keys, how one had gone missing when she had me give it to her friend Adrian. And then a new red one appeared on the ledge in the lobby by the stairs. It was an unsolvable mystery.

Central Park might seem to be the embodiment of controlled wilderness. In fact Olmsted's creation in the middle of Manhattan was not an exercise in taming nature, but rather an act of land reclamation. In the essay "Frederick Law Olmsted and the Dialectical Landscape,"

Smithson considers a "before" photograph included in Olmsted and Vaux's *Greensward Presentation Sketch No. 5*. This photograph reveals a devastated landscape, treeless and barren. Smithson calls it a man-made wasteland. "The site of Central Park was the result of 'urban blight'—trees were cut down by the early settlers without any thought of the future. Such a site could be reclaimed by direct earth-moving without fear of upsetting the ecology."

Smithson compares Central Park to Yosemite National Park. Yosemite did exist in its raw state, an untouched wilderness that did not need to be recycled or improved. The park represents man's effort to change nature in order to accommodate human comfort. "Yosemite is more like an urbanized wilderness with its electrical outlets for campers, and its clothes lines hung between the pines. There is not much room for contemplation in solitude," Smithson writes.

Josefina and the Seminars

Finally Josefina has started her seminars. The topic is Lacan's four fundamental concepts of psychoanalysis. When I walked into the lecture hall in the art department, Hans Holbein the Younger's famous painting *The Ambassadors* was on a screen.

Josefina wore black with a white skirt and plain white shoes. Her round glasses had red frames. She did not put on the bright red lipstick she wears when she speaks with Zizek or Badiou. She told the audience that we could ask questions, to feel free to ask anytime. Then she read from a paper. When I heard the word "burrows," I knew she was talking about William Burroughs and telling the story about the Gysin show at the New Museum. The libido attaches to a part body.

The crutch was leaving Ka stranded at unspecified intervals. She decided it was better to depend on the already lost. So she kept a "person-shaped hole" in the pit of her arm and hobbled through the asphalt lot looking for her old charms.

Pulses could pass
between the magnets
if the lights were on. She
fell around the center and
laughed until it dissolved.

In the "Olmsted" essay, Smithson includes a passage by Uvedale Price, a British baronet and landowner. His writings explored the picturesque, a notion which he located between the beautiful and the sublime.

> The side of a smooth green hill, torn by floods, may at first very properly be called deformed, and on the same principle, though not with the same impression, as a gash on a living animal. When a rawness of such a gash in the ground is softened, and in part concealed and ornamented by the effects of time and the progress of vegetation, deformity, by this usual process, is converted into picturesqueness; and this is the case with quarries, gravel pits, etc., which are at first deformities, and which in their most picturesque state, are often considered as such by a leveling improver.
>
> Uvedale Price, *Three Essays on the Picturesque*, 1810

Vardoger on the Porch

Vardoger arrives to listen to the people on the porch. There are five of them and they are each hooked up to a machine. The sun's rays angle over swells, and hit the riddled buff floorboards. She takes off her helmet and sits down in the middle of the porch. The door must be on the other side. The people don't look at her, they just keep talking. Their brains are hooked up to machines that use electromagnetic stimulation to produce the sense of a presence in their "extrapersonal space." They talk constantly because they are told to record the activities of these presences, their electrically generated doubles.

A man says he feels a woman behind him to the left. Whenever he tries to say something, the woman tells him he will not succeed. If

he does not respond, the woman becomes vicious.
The fleshy arms of a man encircle a woman. She does not want him to stop.

Another woman holds a book. Someone at her side, just out of her peripheral vision, does not want her to open the book. If she begins to read, the woman interrupts her.

A man with a beard tinged blue says: The porch looks over to the shed. Where is the rake? It is in darkness, but the air is warm. Oh, the machines, they roll endless words that pile up and vibrate into the quarry.

Anamorphosis

Holbein's painting *The Ambassadors* was made in the middle of the sixteenth century. The way I remember it, two men in green knickers stand on either side of a table with objects representing geography, music and the arts. In fact, this is not the case. The men are in front of a green brocade curtain and are sartorially well appointed, mostly in black, with special hats and a cape. The objects on the tables include odd globes, a mandolin and enigmatic measuring devices. Art historians debate the identity of these objects and men. What- and whoever they are, the feature that makes this painting so significant is the mottled grayish ellipse on the rug in front of them—it is a skull rendered in anamorphic perspective. Viewing this distorted projection from the front of the painting, the skull is not recognizable. But obliquely, at a specific vantage point, such as when you walk off to the side and turn back for a final look, the skull appears.

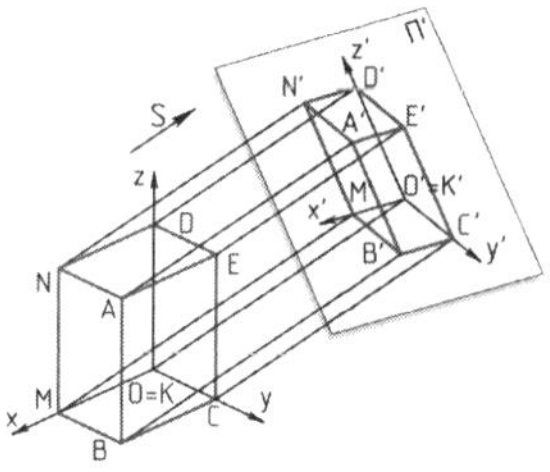

Smithson spends a significant section of the "Olmsted" essay reacting to a column by Grace Glueck in the *New York Times* on the painter Alan Gussow, whose photo appears along with the headline "Artist-in-Residence for Mother Earth." In the article, Gussow accuses the earth artists of cutting and gouging the land like Army engineers, saying that "what's needed are lyric poets to celebrate it." In response Smithson devises his position and that of earth artists, claiming that Gussow fails to recognize the possibility of "a direct organic manipulation of the land devoid of violence and 'macho' aggression." Agriculture, industry and art can each act in the land with an awareness of consequences and an attention to circumstances. "The farmer or engineer who cuts into the land can either cultivate it or devastate it. Representing nature once removed in lyric poetry and landscape painting is not the same as direct cultivation of the land."

Before Smithson reaches this tempered conclusion, he mounts a somewhat ad hominem attack on Gussow. He calls Gussow a mediocre Impressionist painter and his beliefs wishy-washy transcendentalism. He accuses Gussow of being the "type who would rather retreat to scenic beauty spots than try to make a concrete dialectic between nature and people" and says he has an ecological Oedipus complex. Throughout Smithson's critique of Gussow, the influence of psychoanalytic interpretation is apparent, applied not only to Gussow but extended to the earth itself. Smithson refers to Simone de Beauvoir and Theodore Thass-Thienemann, a relatively forgotten figure who wrote books called *The Subconscious Language, Symbolic Behavior,* and *Understanding the Symbolic Meaning of Language.* Smithson illustrates Gussow's "projection of the incest taboo onto nature through penetration of 'Mother Earth'" by quoting a catatonic schizophrenic in Thass-Thienemann's *The Subconscious Language.* As the patient reaches a frenzied state, he shouts, "They should stop digging down inside the earth to draw metals out of it. That's digging down into Mother

Earth and taking things that shouldn't be taken." Yet several paragraphs later Smithson adopts, without irony, similar reasoning: "If strip miners were less alienated from the nature in themselves and free of sexual aggression, cultivation would take place."

Now that she had a mirror for a foot, she saw pieces of herself walking. She asked "Why am I in pieces? I look at others and they seem so complete."

Josefina and the Seminar

She wanted us to understand the difference between looking and seeing—how seeing blinds. She points to the Holbein. When you look at a painting, your eyes dart around inside the picture from place to place. You are searching. You stop looking when you say, "I see," by which you mean that you understand. The images have been transformed into words, the imaginary into the symbolic.

I asked the hoe how to get out. The hoe told me to learn not to fear the end.

Once when Vardoger turned around she saw:

5. the blood patterning the red dress
4. her arms cradling his sliced corpse
3. her tears
2. spikes shooting involuntarily from her fingers
1. her muscleless lover, grinding spices

Her eyes adjust to the dark and she sees a door. Instead of EXIT, it says PEDAGOGICAL SOIL. Approaching she feels a great deal of heat.

Mirror footed Ka straps herself into the egg and remembers pushing the "last man" off the red cliff. How he fell out of sight.

Vardoger occupied the future. Next time she would try for the "present," and from there "explore the pre- and post-historic mind" and "go into places where remote futures meet remote past."

PERSISTENT TRAIT

MARTIN REYNA / LILA ZEMBORAIN

translated by Daniel Coudrier y Mariela Méndez
2011

Secular is
the gesture
of a body
doubled

The rune attenuating
everything
in silhouette

TO skew the other
claiming it
to loosen the tongue
to defame it
ultimately
to strangle it
in the perfect
triangulation
of the stroke

MILLER - ESPINOSA

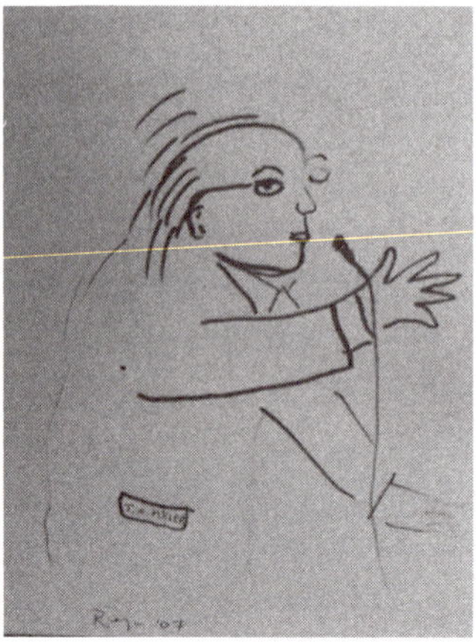

II

Well now
this is the echolalia
the perfect look
of the one atteMpting
sound

Attentive eyes
squeeze everything
in the incidence
of the echo

The instant jumps
behind his back

But the sign
in its verticality
is tempted

III

Were the eye
not to become
strokes
I would say nothing to you

Yet the hand
attemps on the eye
in its declamatIon

Becoming talkative

BeIng that angle

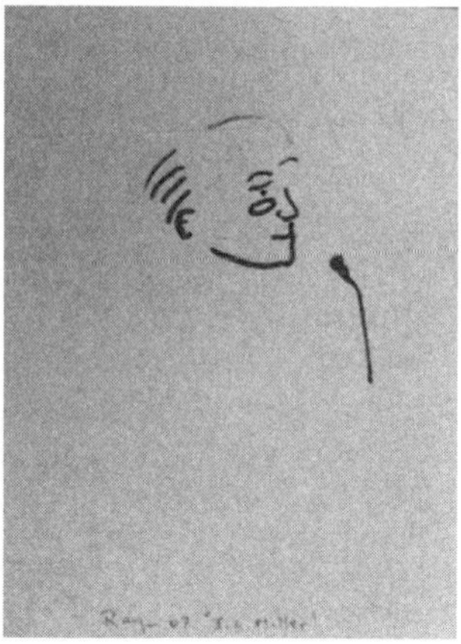

IV

DiscLosure is
that composure

The absence
that announces
a veneration

Being of the other
in that laughter

The lack
ofeye

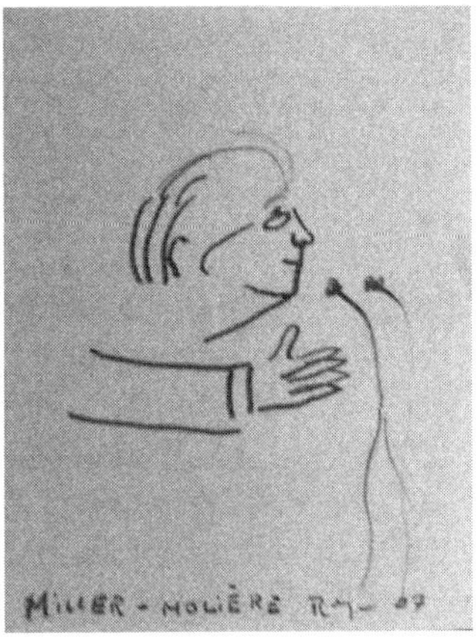

V

It's in turn
this enchantment

This persuasion
that sound
doesn't attenuate

I illuminate
says the hand

Here I am
inclined

But baldness
baLances
the disbelief
on double

ascendedy

VI.

This is the
mirror

This is the
painless trepanation
of the ego

The curve that feeds
the incoherEnce
of the echo

Inclined
the name
holds
everything

VII.

Now it
is instead
the manipulation
of gesture

Hypothetical trait
that moves
everyone

Even the
brain
in its
death rattle
reverbeRates

Persistent trait
of public
consent

Sigmar Polke, *Untitled*, gelatin silver print 24.3 x 19.8 inches, 1964-68/90.

The Grandmother's Voice

Slavoj Zizek

The magic power of voice as object is perhaps best rendered towards the end of the Chapter 1 of Marcel Proust's "The Guermantes Way," a novel which is part of his *In Search Of The Lost Time*.[1] In a memorable scene, using the phone for the first time, Marcel (the narrator of the novel) talks to his grandmother:

> [...] after a few seconds of silence, suddenly I heard that voice which I supposed myself, mistakenly, to know so well; for always until then, every time that my grandmother had talked to me, I had been accustomed to follow what she was saying on the open score of her face, in which the eyes figured so largely; but her voice itself I was hearing this afternoon for the first time. And because that voice appeared to me to have altered in its proportions from the moment that it was a whole, and reached me in this way alone and without the accompaniment of her face and features, I discovered for the first time how sweet that voice was [...]. It was sweet, but also how sad it was, first of all on account of its very sweetness, a sweetness drained almost—more than any but a few human voices can ever have been—of every element of resistance to others, of all selfishness; fragile by reason of its delicacy it seemed at every moment ready to break, to expire in a pure flow of tears; then, too, having it alone beside me, seen, without the mask of her face, I noticed for the first time the sorrows that had scarred it in the course of a lifetime.

What happens here is described by Proust in very precise terms which uncannily point forwards to Lacanian theory: voice is subtracted from its "natural" totality of the body to which it belongs, out of which it emerges as an autonomous partial object, an organ which can magically survive without the body whose organ it is—it is as if it stands "alone beside me, seen, without the mask of her face." This subtraction withdraws it from (our ordinary) reality into the virtual domain of the real, where it persists as an undead specter haunting the subject: "'Granny!' I cried to her, 'Granny!' and would have kissed her, but I had beside me only that voice, a phantom, as impalpable as that which would come perhaps to revisit me when my grandmother was dead." As such, this voice signals simultaneously a distance (granny is not here) and an obscene over-proximity, a presence more intimate, more penetrating, than that of an external body in front of us:

> A real presence indeed that voice so near—in actual separation. But a premonition also of an eternal separation! Over and again, as I listened in this way, without seeing her who spoke to me from so far away, it has seemed to me that the voice was crying to me from depths out of which one does not rise again, and I have known the anxiety that was one day to wring my heart when a voice should thus return (alone, and attached no longer to a body which I was never more to see).

The term "anxiety" is to be read in the precise Lacanian way: for Lacan, anxiety does not signal the loss of the object, but, on the contrary, its over-proximity. Anxiety arises when the *objet a* directly falls into reality, appears in it—which is precisely what happens when Marcel hears the granny's voice separated from her body and discovers "for the first time how sweet that voice was": this sweetness is, of course, the extracted quintessence which made granny so heavily libidinally invested. This, incidentally, is how psychoanalysis approaches the libidinal-subjective impact of new technological inventions: "technology is a catalizer, it enlarges and enhances something which is already here"[2]—in this case, a fantasmatic virtual fact, like that of a partial object. (Something like this happens in a psychoanalytic session where, precisely, the patient is reduced to a voice: "psychoanalysis makes out of the ordinary voice a telephone voice."[3]) And, of course, this realization changes the entire constellation: once a fantasy is realized, once a fantasmatic object directly appears in reality, reality is no longer the same. Recall the industry of sex-gadgets: one finds today on the market a so-called "Stamina Training Unit," a masturbatory device which resembles a battery light (so that, when we carry it around, we are not embarrassed): you put the erected penis into the opening at the top and move the thing up and down till satisfaction... The product is available in different colors, tightness, and forms that imitate all three main openings for sexual penetration (mouth, vagina, anus). What one buys here is simply the partial object (erogenous zone) alone, deprived of the embarrassing additional burden of the entire person. The fantasy (of reducing the sexual partner to a partial object) is here directly realized, and this changes the entire libidinal economy of sexual relations.

This brings us to the key question: what happens to the body when it is separated from its voice, when the voice is subtracted from the wholeness of the person? For a brief moment, we see "a world robbed of fantasy, of the affective frame and sense, a world out of joint."[4] Grandmother appears to Marcel outside the fantasmatic horizon of meaning, the rich texture of his previous long experience of her, which up till now made her a warm charming person—all of a sudden, he sees her "red-faced, heavy and common, sick, lost in thought, following the lines of a book with eyes that seemed hardly sane, a dejected old woman whom I did not know." Perhaps the best metaphor is here that of a squid which moves elegantly in water, but turns into a disgusting helpless peace of slimy meat once out of water: seen after the fateful phone conversation, deprived of her fantasy frame, granny is like a squid outside water, on dry land—here is Proust's precise description of this effect:

[...] when, entering the drawing-room before my grandmother had been told of my return, I found her there, reading. I was in the room, or rather I was not yet in the room since she was not aware of my presence, and, like a woman whom one surprises at a piece of work which she will lay aside if anyone comes in, she had abandoned herself to a train of thoughts which she had never allowed to be visible by me. Of myself—thanks to that privilege which does not last but which one enjoys during the brief moment of return, the faculty of being a spectator, so to speak, of one's own absence,—there was present only the witness, the observer, with a hat and traveling coat, the stranger who does not belong to the house, the photographer who has called to take a photograph of places which one will never see again. The process that mechanically occurred in my eyes when I caught sight of my grandmother was indeed a photograph. We never see the people who are dear to us save in the animated system, the perpetual motion of our incessant love for them, which before allowing the images that their faces present to reach us catches them in its vortex, flings them back upon the idea that we have always had of them, makes them adhere to it, coincide with it. [...] But if, in place of our eye, it should be a purely material object, a photographic plate, that has watched the action, then what we shall see, in the courtyard of the Institute, for example, will be, instead of the dignified emergence of an Academician who is going to hail a cab, his staggering gait, his precautions to avoid tumbling upon his back, the parabola of his fall, as though he were drunk, or the ground frozen over. So is it when some casual sport of chance prevents our intelligent and pious affection from coming forward in time to hide from our eyes what they ought never to behold, when it is forestalled by our eyes, and they, arising first in the field and having it to themselves, set to work mechanically, like films, and show us, in place of the loved friend who has long ago ceased to exist but whose death our affection has always hitherto kept concealed from us, the new person whom a hundred times daily that affection has clothed with a dear and cheating likeness. [...] I, for whom my grandmother was still myself, I who had never seen her save in my own soul, always at the same place in the past, through the transparent sheets of contiguous, overlapping memories, suddenly in our drawing-room which formed part of a new world, that of time, that in which dwell the strangers of whom

> we say 'He's begun to age a good deal,' for the first time and for a moment only, since she vanished at once, I saw, sitting on the sofa, beneath the lamp, red-faced, heavy and common, sick, lost in thought, following the lines of a book with eyes that seemed hardly sane, a dejected old woman whom I did not know.

One should read this passage against its implicit Kantian background: a network screens our raw perceptions of beloved persons, i.e.,

> before allowing the images that their faces present to reach us catches them in its vortex, [it] flings them back upon the idea that we have always had of them, makes them adhere to it, coincide with it;

this network—the complex web of past experiences, affections, etc., which colors our raw perceptions—plays exactly the role of a transcendental horizon which makes our reality meaningful. When we are deprived of this transcendental network, i.e., of the fantasmatic coordinates of meaning, we are no longer engaged participants in the world, we find ourselves confronted with things in their noumenal dimension: for a moment, we see them the way they are "in themselves," independently of us—or, as Proust puts it in a wonderful formula, the spectator becomes "a spectator, so to speak, of one's own absence." What this means is that, once the fantasy-object is subtracted from reality, it is not only the observed reality which changes, but also the observing subject himself: he is reduced to a gaze observing how things look in his own absence (recall the old Tom-Sawyer-and-Huck-Finn fantasy of being present at one's own funeral). And is this, precisely, not the feature which makes the photographic camera so uncanny? Is a camera not our eye separated from our body, drifting around and recording how things look in our absence?

Deleuze often varies the motif of how, in becoming post-human, we should learn to practice "a perception as it was before men (or after) [...] released from their human coordinates"[5]: those who fully endorse the Nietzschean "return of the same" are strong enough to sustain the vision of the "iridescent chaos of a world before man."[6] Although Deleuze resorts here openly to Kant's language, talking about the direct access to "things (the way they are) in themselves," his point is precisely that one should subtract the opposition between phenomena and things-in-themselves, between the phenomenal and the nolumenal level, from its Kantian functioning, where noumena are transcendent things that forever elude our grasp. What Deleuze refers to as "things in themselves" is in a way *even more phenomenal* then our shared phenomenal reality: it is the impossible phenomenon, the phenomenon that is excluded from our symbolically-constituted reality. The gap that separates us from noumena is thus primarily not epistemological, but practico-ethical and libidinal: there is no "true reality" behind or beneath phenomena, noumena are phenomenal things which are "too strong," too intens(iv)e, for our perceptual apparatus attuned to constituted reality—epistemological failure is a secondary effect of libidinal terror, i.e., the underlying logic is a reversal of Kant's "You can, because you must!" "You cannot (know nolumena), because you must not!" Imagine someone being forced to witness a terrifying torture: in a way, the monstrosity of what he saw would make this an experience of the noumenal impossible-real that would shatter the coordinates of our common reality. (The same holds for witnessing an intense sexual activity.) In this sense, if we were to discover films shot in a concentration camp among the *Musulmannen*, showing scenes from their daily life, how they are systematically mistreated and deprived of all dignity, we would have "seen too much," the prohibited, we would have entered a forbidden territory of what should have remained unseen. (One can well understand Claude Lanzmann who said that, if he were to stumble upon such a film, he would have destroyed it immediately.) This is also what makes it so unbearable to witness the last moments of people who know they are shortly going to die and are in this sense already living-dead—again, imagine that we would have discovered, among the ruins of the Twin Towers, a video camera that magically survived the crash intact and is full of shots of what went on among the passengers of the plane in the minutes before it crashed into one of the Towers. In all these cases, it is that, effectively, we would have seen things as they are "in themselvers," outside human coordinates, outside our human reality—we would have seen the world with inhuman eyes. (Maybe the US authorities do possess such shots and, for understandable reasons, are keeping them secret.) The lesson is here profoundly Hegelian: the difference between the phenomenal and the noumenal has to be reflected/transposed back into the phenomenal, as the split between the "gentrified" normal phenomenon and the "impossible" phenomenon.

So, to recapitulate: the grandmother's voice, heard alone, apart from her body, surprises Marcel—it is the voice of a frail old woman, not the voice of the grandmother he remembers. And the point is that this experience colors his perception of the grandmother: when, later, he visits her in person, he perceives her in a new way, as a strange mad old woman drowsing over her book, overburdened with age, flushed and course, no longer the charming and caring grandmother he remembered. This is how voice as autonomous partial object can affect our entire perception of the body to which it belongs. The lesson of it is that, precisely, the direct experience of the unity of a body, where voice seems to fit its organic whole, involves a necessary mystification; in order to penetrate to the truth, one has to tear this unity apart, to focus onto one of its aspects in its isolation, and then to allow this element to color our entire perception. In other words, what we find here is another case of Freud's anti-hermeneutic motto: one should interpret en detail, not en masse. To locate every feature of a human being into the organic Whole of the person is to miss not only its meaning, but the true meaning of the Whole itself. In this sense also, person and subject are to be opposed: subject is de-centered with regard to person, it obtains its minimal consistency from a singular feature ("partial object").

This object is what Lacan referred to as *objet petit a*, the object-cause of desire, and what its paradoxes indicate is that, in *objet a*, form and content coincide: *objet a* is the "indivisible remainder" which escapes the symbolic form, and, simultaneously, pure form, a purely formal distortion (protraction, etc.) of the content. More precisely, this oscillation of *objet a* between form and content involves four consecutive dialectical reversals, a kind of complex negation of negation. It is symptomatic how, when Lacan and his followers articulate something that clearly has the structure of the "negation of negation," they almost compulsively hasten to add that this is not meant in the Hegelian sense—is this not a defense mechanism par excellence, the disavowal of an uncomfortable proximity? How, then, does it stand with "negation of negation" in Lacan? Is it compatible with Hegel's? Since, in Lacan, in a (seeming) contrast to Hegel, the double movement of "negation of negation" produces an excess/remainder, that of the *objet a*, let us begin with Miller who, in his commentary on Lacan's Seminar XVI, elaborated the crucial change in the status of *objet petit a*, the object-cause of desire: the passage from corporeal specimen (partial object: breast, faeces…) to a pure logical function; in this seminar,

> Lacan does not really describe *objets a* as corporeal specimens, he constructs them as a logical consistency, logic being there in the place of biology. The logical consistency is like a function that the body must satisfy through different bodily deductions.[7]

This passage is the passage from the foreign intruder, the pieces of sand heterogeneous to the signifying machine, preventing its smooth functioning, to the total homogeneity to this machine. When Lacan is describing the loops and twists of the symbolic space on account of which its interiority overlaps with its exteriority ("ex-timacy"), he does not merely describe the structural place of *objet a* (surplus-enjoyment): surplus-enjoyment is *nothing but this structure itself*, this "inward loop" of the symbolic space. Let us clarify this with the gap that separates drive from instinct: while drive and instinct the same "object," the same goal, what differentiates them is that drive finds satisfaction not in reaching its goal, but in circulating around it, repeating the failure to reach it. One can say, of course, that what prevents the drive from reaching its goal is the *objet a* which is decentered with regard to it, so that, even if we reach the goal, the object eludes us and we are condemned to repeat the procedure; however, this *objet a* is purely formal, it is the curvature of the space of drive on account of which the "shortest way" to reach the object is not to aim directly at it but to encircle it, to tour around it.

This shift is deeply Hegelian, it forms a kind of "negation of negation": first, we have the consistent "big Other," the self-enclosed symbolic order; then, in the first negation, this consistency is disturbed by the remainder of the real, a traumatic left-over which resists being integrated into the symbolic and thus disturbs its balance, rendering it "barred," introducing into it a gap, flaw, antagonism, in short, inconsistency; in the second negation, however, one is compelled to accomplish a kind of shift of perspective and grasp this very intruding left-over of the real as the only element that guarantees the minimal consistency of the inconsistent big Other. Recall the logic of class struggle: class struggle renders society "inconsistent," antagonistic, perturbing its balanced hierarchy; however, it is simultaneously that which holds the entire social body together, its underlying structuring principle, since all social phenomena are overdetermined by class struggle. At a more prosaic level, is it not often that the very struggle, tension, is what keeps elements together? When struggle disappears, elements drift apart in sterile indifferent co-existence. In the same way, trauma is, of course, that which disturbs the balance of the subject's symbolic space; however, it is simultaneously the ultimate point of reference of this subject's psychic life—all his symbolizing activity ultimately aims at coping with the trauma, repressing it, displacing it, etc.

There is even more to this: not only does this intruding element "keep together" the big Other who, in the absence of this intruder, would have fallen apart; this element, *objet a*, has no positive objectal reality, its status is purely that of logical consistency: it is logically implied, presupposed, as the cause of the inconsistencies of/in the big Other, i.e., it can only be discerned retroactively, through its effects. Let us take an attractor in mathematics: all positive lines or points in its sphere of attraction only approach it in an endless fashion, never reaching its form—the existence of this form is purely virtual, being nothing more than the shape towards which lines and points tend. However, precisely as such, the virtual is the real of this field: the immovable focal point around which all elements circulate.

The Hegelian logic of these twists can thus be rendered even more precise: there are not only three, but four moments at work here. First, the consistent big Other; then, the big Other rendered inconsistent by the object a as intruding remainder; then, this object as the very object that guarantees the "consistency" of the big Other (the multiple inconsistent symbolizations can only be "totalized" as a texture of reactions to the intruding object); finally, we are back at the beginning, although at a different level—there is no object that, from outside, perturbs the consistency of the big Other, the object a as the "real" is only a name for the purely formal twist, internal loop, of the symbolic order itself.

Is, then, the *objet a*, insofar as it lacks its mirror image, the vampiric object (vampires, as we know, do not generate their image in a mirror)? It may seem so: are vampires not versions of *lamella*, of the undead partial object? However, perhaps the exact opposite is more appropriate as an image of *objet a*: when we look at a thing directly, in reality, we don't see "it"—this "it" only appears when we look at the thing's mirror image, as if there is, in the mirror image, something more than in reality, as if only the mirror image can bring out the mysterious ingredient for which we search in vain in the object's reality. Or, to put it in Deleuzian terms: the mirror image desubstantializes a thing, depriving it of its density and depth, reducing it to a flat surface, and it is only through this reduction that the purely non-substantial *objet a* becomes perceptible.[8]

Perhaps, this double status of *objet a* also provides a clue for the relationship between death drive and superego. Some time ago, Eric Santner raised a critical point about my work:

> The link, even at times identity, in your work, of the organ without body and the superego. Should we just collapse the superego and the death drive like this? Doesn't everything depend on keeping at least a thin line between them? Shouldn't we speak of a superegoization of drive?[9]

As Santner emphasizes, we are dealing with a parallax split, not with the cosmic polarity of two opposed forced: OwB and superego are not like yin and yang or light and dark principle. Furthermore, the tension we are dealing with is asymmetric, the two poles are not balanced, the OwB aspect somehow has priority—but what exact kind of priority? What one should reject is the notion that we are dealing with yet another case of the logic of self-alienation at work from Marx and Nietzsche to Deleuze, of a generative power which misrecognizes itself in its own product: in the same way that, say, for Marx, capital is the result of collective labor turned against itself, its own origin, or, for Nietzsche, moral resentment is the productivity of life turned against itself, the superego excess is the excess of the OwB turned against itself; along these lines, the task would have been to reduce the alienated result back to its origin, i.e., to establish the reign of the excess of OwB without its superego distortion... This, however, is the very logic one should avoid at any cost. (A direct reference to the formulas of sexuation [the "masculine" superego versus the "feminine" drive] also has its limits.)

One of the paths to pursue here is to link this duality of superego and drive to the duality in the status of *objet petit a*: is "superego" as the first name for the excess of drive not the object in its aspect of material reality, of the foreign intruder that "drives me crazy" with its impossible requests, and is the OwB not the object in its aspect of a purely formal structure? Both aspects display the same self-propelling twisted structure of a loop: the more the subject obeys the superego, the more he is guilty, caught in the repetitive movement which is formally the same as that of the drive circulating around its object. The passage from the first to the second aspect is structurally homologous to that of the Rabinovitch joke, of the problem which is its own solution: what, at the level of the superego, appears as a deadlock (the more I obey, the more I am guilty…), turns into the very source of satisfaction (which is not the object of the drive, but the very activity of repeatedly encircling it).[10] (And does the same shift not determine also the status of the Badiouian Event with regard to how it relates to the order of Being? An Event inscribes itself into the order of Being, leaving its traces in it, "or rather" an Event is NOTHING BUT a certain distortion/twist in the order of Being. The four stages in the development of *objet a* can effectively be applied to Event in its relation to Being: first, there is the order of Being; then, this order is rendered incomplete/inconsistent by the miracle of an Event; then, this event appears as the virtual point of consistency which only renders readable the inconsistently distorted texture of Being; finally, Event appears as NOTHING BUT this distortion of Being.) Perhaps this reference to Lacan also enables us to formulate the moment that is missing in Badiou's scheme: is it not possible to think this distortion of Being independently of (or as prior to) the Event, so that "Event" ultimately names a minimal "fetishization" of the immanent distortion of the texture of Being into its virtual object-cause? And is the Freudo-Lacanian name of this distortion not DRIVE, death drive? So, back to the two aspects of *objet a*, its corporeal reality and logical consistency: although antinomic, they fit together—but how, exactly? Miller's first formulation is that of a hole (empty place) and the contingent element filling it in:

> The small a, when it is designated as topological structure and as logical consistency, has, if I may say so, the substance of a hole, and then some detached pieces of the body are moulded in this absence.[11]

Is, however, this formulation not all too simplistic? Does the paradox of an object which "is" only its formal structure not disappear here? How, then, are we to accomplish the step which, in the terms of the classical Teachers, one could call the step from metaphysical/mechanical to dialectical materialism? In his *Logic of Sense*, Deleuze provided a model allowing us to grasp the mediation of form and content when he developed how the two series (of the signifier and the signified) always contain a paradoxical entity that is "doubly inscribed" (i.e., that is simultaneously surplus and lack): a surplus of the signifier over the signified (the empty signifier without a signified) and the lack of the signified (the point of nonsense within the field of Sense). That is to say, as soon as the symbolic order emerges, we are dealing with the minimal difference between a structural place and the element that occupies, fills out, this place: an element is always logically preceded by the place in the structure it fills out. The two series can, therefore, also be described as the "empty" formal structure (signifier) and the series of elements filling out the empty places in the structure (signified). From this perspective, the paradox consists in the fact that the two series never overlap: we always encounter an entity that is simultaneously—with regard to the structure—an empty, unoccupied place and—with regard to the elements—a rapidly moving, elusive object, an occupant without a place. We have thereby produced Lacan's formula of the fantasm $\$ <> a$, since the matheme for the subject is $\$$, an empty place in the structure, an elided signifier, while *objet a* is, by definition, an excessive object, an object that lacks its place in the structure. Consequently, the point is not that there is simply the surplus of an element over the places available in the structure or the surplus of a place that has no element to fill it out. An empty place in the structure would still sustain the fantasy of an element that will emerge and fill out this place; an excessive element lacking its place would still sustain the fantasy of some yet unknown place waiting for it. The point is, rather, that the empty place in the structure is strictly correlative to the errant element lacking its place: they are not two different entities, but the front and the back of one and the same entity, that is, one and the same entity inscribed onto the two surfaces of a Moebius strip. In short, the subject qua $\$$ doesn't belong to the depth: it emerges from a topological twist of the surface itself. Does Miller himself not point in this direction later in the same text?

> When Lacan speaks of a hole at the level of the big Other, he must say that the hole is not a lack, but it is what permits, on the contrary, in Lacan's logical elucubrations, the interior circle of the Other to be considered as conjoined to the most exterior circle, almost as its inversion. Lacan says in passing that it is the structure itself of the *objet a*, or rather that the *objet a* is this structure in which the most interior is conjoined to the most exterior in its turning.[12]

The "or rather" has to be given its whole weight here: from the structure OF the object to a strange object which IS nothing but this structure, its substantial identity merely a reified specter. This object "is" subject, i.e., the subject's impossible/real objectal correlate. This weird correlation subverts the standard transcendental correlation between subject and object: in it, the subject is correlated with the very impossible/real object that has to be excluded from the field of reality so that the subject can relate to this field. In order to delineate this unique character of *objet a* as the embodiment of a void, of the lack/loss of the primordial object which can only emerge as always-already lost, Lacan opposes it to two other figures of nothingness, the nothingness of destruction and the Hegelian negativity which is the "nullification" constitutive of subjectivity, the nothing as the initial moment in the instauration of the subject; in contrast to these two versions, he

relates *objet a* to what Kant called *der Gegenstand ohne Begriff*, the object without concept (not covered by any concept). *Objet a* is as such "irrational," in the strictly literal sense of outside all ratio, all relation as proportion. In other words, when a particular element resists being subsumed under a universal concept, *objet a*, "what is in you more than yourself," is precisely *that je ne sais quoi* which prevents this subsumption. Here, however, one must remain a consequent Hegelian and resist the empiricist temptation:

SIGMAR POLKE, *Untitled*, Photograph on Agfa-Gevaert Copyline Projection, 8.3 x 11.4 inches, 1969-70.

the fact that the assertion of the existence of a particular element goes against the universal notion supposed to cover/contain this element should not be dismissed as the case of the wealth of the particular content overwhelming abstract notional frameworks; the empirical excess should rather be read as an indication of the inherent inconsistency/failure of the universal notion itself. So when Lacan says that "only with the analytic discourse can a universal find its true ground in the existence of an exception, which is why it is sure that we can in any case distinguish the universal which is thus grounded from all use of this same universal rendered common by the philosophical tradition"(*...ou pire*, March 3 1972), he (as usual) ignores the uniqueness of the Hegelian "concrete universality." Why not risk even a political example here? When, in order to install hope among radical Leftist, some intellectuals point out that there exists today some authentic emancipator agent (usually far away, in Haiti or Venezuela or Nepal...), this triumphant assertion ("You see, we are not dreaming, there is an authentic revolutionary process going on!") serves precisely as a fetish enabling us to avoid the confrontation with the inadequacy of the standard notion of radical emancipator agent for today's global struggle. What this means is that, in the opposition between concept and reality (real existence), *objet a* is on the side of the concept: it is not the excess of reality, but an immanent hole or crack in the conceptual edifice.

Objet a is thus not the core of reality which resists being subsumed by the conceptual frame imposed by the subject; it is, on the contrary, the objectivization of the subject's desire: the status of that which makes me desire an object is irreducibly linked to my "subjective" perspective, it is not simply an objective property of the beloved—that *x* which fascinates me in the beloved exists only for me, not for an "objective" view. One can even go a step further and argue that subjective mediation is here double: far from simply standing for the excess in the object eluding the subject's grasp, *objet a* is, at its most elementary, what I see in the other's gaze. In other words, what eludes me in a libidinal object is not some transcendent property but the inscription into it of my own desire: what I see in the other is his/her desire for me, i.e., I read in his/her eyes my own status as that of an object (of desire), the way I appear to the other.

1. Available online at http://ebooks.adelaide.edu.au/p/proust/marcel/p96g/chapter1a.html.
2. Mladen Dolar, "Telephone and Psychoanalysis," Filozofski vestnik, Ljubljana (in Slovene), No. 1/2008, p. 12; I rely here heavily on this text.
3. Op.cit., p. 22.
4. Op.cit., p. 11.
5. Gilles Deleuze, *L'image-mouvement*, Paris: Editions de Minuit 1983, p.122.
6. Op.cit., p. 81.
7. Jacques-Alain Miller, "A Reading of the Seminar From an Other to the other," *lacanian ink* 29, New York 2007, p. 13.
8. One of the stories in the classic British horror omnibus *Dead of Night* plays on this very register: a couple moves into a renovated house with an old large mirror in their living room; when, in the evening, the husband looks into the mirror, he sees in it a scene totally different from the reality of the living room, an old-fashioned room with a fireplace. The explanation is that, two centuries ago, a terrible murder happened in this very room, which is »remembered« by the mirror.
9. Private communication.
10. According to Freud, love arises out of the inhibited desire: the object whose (sexual) consummation is prevented is then idealized into a love object. This is why Lacan establishes a link between love and drive: the space of drive is defined by the gap between its goal (object) and its aim, which is not to directly reach its object, but to circulate around the object, to repeat the failure to reach it—what drive and love share is this structure of inhibition.
11. Miller, op.cit., p. 25.
12. Op.cit., p. 18.

Martin Kippenberg, Sigmar Polke

Cathy Lebowitz interviews JA

Cathy Lebowitz: The sculpture of Kippenberger's man in a moving chair, in his suit, with his plastic face, reminds me of Zizek's discussion of Lacan's idea of appearances. Appearance at its purest "occurs not when we put up a deceiving screen to conceal the transgression, but when we fake that there is a transgression to be concealed." Who is this man? What is he hiding?

Josefina Ayerza: As for Kippenberger's man in a moving chair, in his suit, with his plastic face... if faking a transgression to be concealed, he may no longer pretend he doesn't know what everyone knows he knows because his thoughts are visible—inside his transparent head. To a point that everybody can see it, something in the shape of a body stands in between his eyes... The feet on the man's mouth, if the figure sitting in place of his nose is a woman, she could well fit Lacan's concept about the woman being the symptom of man.

Martin Kippenberger, "I Had A Vision," installation view at Luhring Augustine Gallery, 2011

CL: Can you remind me how the woman is a symptom of the man?

JA: Because man structures his life around her—woman. In other words, Symptom is that around which you structure your life.

CL: So this thing between his eyes, it could be a woman or something else. But it does seem that he could not escape structuring his life around it. Maybe that is why he must ride locked to a track. Do you think the fact that he does not stand on his feet but sits on this cart has a meaning?

JA: What makes it mandatory, is the fact that the stain—be it desire, the phallus, a fantasy or the object... should be guiding him. Even if fantasy is not a sexual rapport, but a making-up for a sexual rapport; it is the relation between a subject and an object. So here, the object—an *objet a* which is causing, determining desire—comes in place of the Other sex, an Other that rides locked to a track because his becoming is being manipulated.

CL: Are you saying: It is mandatory because the stain should be guiding him? In this case, who is the "he" and who is the Other? It sounds like they are both the man.

JA: The Other belongs in the register of being, which is multiplicity: much as you come to recognize the actual desire as your own it will invest another body... The problem with the actual man guiding the track, both the "he" and the "Other", is not that the desire impelling him is phallic, but that there is only one. Then if there is only one Other, only one phallus, only one fantasy... the sole object, obsessive as star wallpaper, there is only one unconscious. Not a feminine unconscious or masculine unconscious, if there is only One, a feminine unconscious and a masculine one are not discernable. It follows that there is but one sexuality and only one discourse, as sexuality is located in the field of discourse.

"Sexuality for human beings," says Lacan, "is nothing but semblant, nothing but make-believe."

CL: Is this what Lacan means when he says "There is no sexual relation"?

JA: In the "Meaning of the Phallus"—*Écrits*, it was all about making two distinctive positions out of one sex. So to Freud's traditional combinatory: "negation, to have, to be," Lacan appends the phallus as signifier. Ten years later—in Seminar XX, *Encore*—it is precisely the phallus as axis of symmetry that he will drop. Sexual difference is no longer organized in a symmetrical way; Lacan moves on from Freud.

MARTIN KIPPENBERGER, *Untitled (wallpaper)*, offset print, 59.5 x 72.8 cm (each), 1991.

MARTIN KIPPENBERGER, *Untitled*, electromobile, remote control, cast resin, plastic, metal, foam plastic, clothing with ramp: chipboard, wood, paint (grey), 98 1/2 x 49 1/4," 1991.

CL: What about Polke's photographs of dead couples? There is no sexual relation there.

JA: Indeed, there is no sexual relation between corpses. Here the famous difference between the sexes has altogether vanished. Not so *jouissance*, in any event clinging to the morals.

And it is against this background that we may locate Dostoyevsky's dubious statement: "If God doesn't exist, then everything is permitted." In "Bobok," an alcoholic literary man named Ivan Ivanovich is suffering from auditory hallucinations: "I am beginning to see and hear strange things, not voices exactly, but as though someone beside me were muttering, 'bobok, bobok, bobok!'" He goes out in search of diversion, and hits upon a funeral. He attends the funeral and remains in the cemetery. "I began to hear things being said, of all sorts. At first I did not

SIGMAR POLKE, *Untitled (Palermo)*, gelatin silver print, 29.5 x 32.7," 1976.

pay attention, treated it with contempt. The conversation went on. I heard muffled sounds as though the speakers' mouths were covered with a pillow, at the same time that distinct and very near. I came to myself, sat up and began listening attentively."

He discovers that human consciousness goes on for some time after the death of the physical body, lasting until total decomposition. One of the deceased characters comments:

"The great thing is that we have two or three months more of life and then—bobok! I propose to spend these two months as agreeably as possible, Gentlemen! I propose to cast aside all shame."

SIGMAR POLKE, *Untitled (Palermo)*, gelatin silver print, 32.7 x 29.5," 1976.

The dead, realizing their complete freedom from earthly conditions, decide to entertain themselves by telling tales of their existence during their lives:

"I don't want us to be telling lies. That's all I care about, for that is one thing that matters. One cannot exist on the surface without lying, for life and lying are synonymous, but here we will amuse ourselves by not lying. Hang it all, the grave has some value after all! We'll all tell our stories aloud, and we won't be ashamed of anything. First of all I'll tell you about myself. I am one of the predatory kind, you know—all was bound and held in check by rotten cords up there on the surface. Away with cords and let us spend these two months in shameless truthfulness! Let us strip and be naked! Let us be naked, let us be naked! cried all the voices."

And here I suddenly sneezed. It happened suddenly and unintentionally, but the effect was striking: all became as silent as one expects it to be in a churchyard, it all vanished like a dream. A real silence of the tomb set in. I don't believe they were ashamed on account of my presence: they had made up their minds to cast off all shame! I waited five minutes—not a word, not a sound."

"Bobok," as the quintessence of Dostoyevsky's art, is a microcosm which renders its central motif: the idea that "everything is permitted" if there is no God and no immortality of the soul. However, and to pursue the discussion with Zizek, this is Dostoyevsky's mistake. "In the carnivalesque underworld of life "between the two deaths," all rules and responsibilities are suspended, the undead can cast aside all shame, act insanely, and laugh at honesty and justice. The ethical horror of this vision is that it displays the limit of the "truth and reconciliation" idea: what if we have a perpetrator for whom the public confession of his crimes not only does not give rise to any ethical catharsis in him, but even generates an additional obscene pleasure?

The "undead" situation of the deceased is opposed to that

of the father from one of the dreams reported by Freud, who goes on living because he doesn't know that he is dead. The deceased in Dostoyevsky's story are fully aware that they are dead—it is this awareness that allows them to cast away all shame. So what is the secret the deceased carefully conceal from every mortal? The talking corpses experience their life after (biological) death, which is in itself a proof of God's existence—God is here, keeping them alive after death, which is why they can say everything."

What Dostoyevsky stages is a religious phantasy which has nothing whatsoever to do with a truly atheist position—although he stages it to illustrate the godless universe in which "everything is permitted." So what is the compulsion that pushes the corpses to engage in the sincerity of "saying it all?" The Lacanian answer is superego—not as the ethical agency, but as a a naughty injunction to *jouir.*

SIGMAR POLKE, *Untitled (Palermo)*, gelatin silver print, 29.5 x 32.7," 1976.

Photo: Egan Frantz

The Symptom

12

après-coup
objet a
fantasm
Other (A)
surmoitié
jouissance
plus-de-jouir
imaginary
symbolic
real

http://www.lacan.com

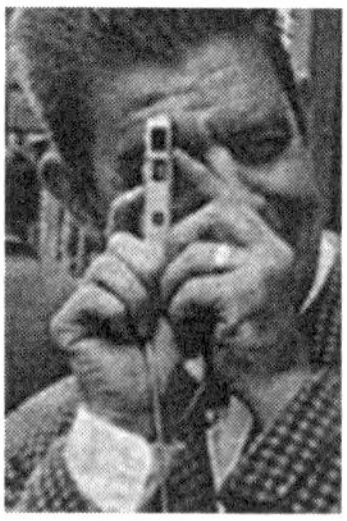

Josefina Ayerza

"Four Fundamental Concepts of Psychoanalysis"

•Fall 2011 at 7:30 pm

• JLW - Jacques Lacan Workshop

NYU Steinhardt Art
34 Stuyvesant Street
New York, NY 10003

certainty
A | O (A)
T | P

SUBSCRIBE TO *lacanian ink*

For one year subscription (2 issues) to *lacanian ink* please send check or money order payable in US dollars.

Institutional Subscription	—	$65.00
Individual Subscription	—	$30.00

Postage and handling:

Outside the U.S.	—	$22.00
Canada	—	$12.00

The following back issues are available at $20.00 per copy to individuals and $45.00 to institutions.

1 ☐ 2 ☐ 3 ☐ 4 ☐ 5 ☐ 8 ☐

9 ☐ 11 ☐ 12 ☐ 15 ☐ 17 ☐ 18 ☐

31 ☐ 32 ☐ 33 ☐ 34 ☐ 35 ☐ 36 ☐

Issues 6, 7, 10, 13, 14, 16, 19, 20, 21, 22, 23, 24/25, 26, 27, 28, 29 and 30 are out of print.

Name ______________________________

Address ______________________________

City ______________________________

State & Zip ______________________________

Mail to:
lacanian ink
133 Wooster Street
New York, NY 10012

over the internet:
www.lacan.com/form.htm
e-mail:
lacink@lacan.com